Photographs and photography in Irish local history

Maynooth Research Guides for Irish Local History

GENERAL EDITOR Mary Ann Lyons

This book is one of the Maynooth Research Guides for Irish Local History series. Written by specialists in the relevant fields, these volumes are designed to provide historians, and especially those interested in local history, with practical advice regarding the consultation of specific collections of historical materials, thereby enabling them to conduct independent research in a competent and thorough manner. In each volume, a brief history of the relevant institutions is provided and the principal primary sources are identified and critically evaluated with specific reference to their usefulness to the local historian. Readers receive step by step guidance as to how to conduct their research and are alerted to some of the problems which they might encounter in working with particular collections. Possible avenues for research are suggested and relevant secondary works are also recommended.

The General Editor acknowledges the assistance of both Professor Raymond Gillespie, NUI Maynooth and Dr James Kelly, St Patrick's College, Drumcondra, in the preparation of this book for publication.

IN THIS SERIES

Maynooth Research Guides for Irish Local History: Number 13

Photographs and photography in Irish local history

Liam Kelly

FOUR COURTS PRESS

Set in 10.5 pt on 12.5 pt Bembo by
Carrigboy Typesetting Services for
FOUR COURTS PRESS LTD
7 Malpas Street, Dublin 8
e-mail: info@fourcourtspress.ie
www.fourcourtspress.ie
and in North America by
FOUR COURTS PRESS
c/o ISBS, 920 N.E. 58th Avenue, Suite 300, Portland, OR 97213

A catalogue record for this title
is available from the British Library.

ISBN 978–1–84682–125–7 hbk
978–1–84682–126–4 pbk

SPECIAL ACKNOWLEDGMENT

This publication was grant-aided by the Heritage Council
under the 2008 Publication grant scheme

AN
CHOMHAIRLE
OIDHREACHTA

THE
HERITAGE
COUNCIL

Printed in England
by MPG Books Ltd, Bodmin, Cornwall.

Contents

Illustrations

Acknowledgments

My earliest debt of gratitude is to Elizabeth Mans. When I visited her in west Cork in 1983 she entrusted me with a wonderful collection of photographs taken by her granduncle, Leland Lewis Duncan, in Co. Leitrim between 1889 and 1894. That collection fostered my interest in photographs and convinced me that they were a very useful and underused primary source for local historians.

In more recent times I am indebted to many people. In particular I wish to thank Mary Ann Lyons, the general editor of this series, who was involved with this guide from the beginning and who was always courteous and helpful and showed immense patience and skill in editing this work. My thanks also to Professor Raymond Gillespie of NUI Maynooth. His enthusiasm for local history is infectious and it was he who encouraged me to write this guide.

I am also indebted to Sara Smyth, the assistant keeper of the National Photographic Archive, for all her help and advice. She supplied me with information about the photographic collections which the Archive acquired in recent years and which are not listed in Sara Rouse's *Into the light, an illustrated guide to the photographic collections in the National Library of Ireland*. Chris Corlett gave me details on the photographic collections held by the Royal Society of Antiquaries of Ireland. I wish to thank him and many other people – librarians, curators and local studies personnel – for giving me information on the photographic collections held in libraries, archives and museums throughout the country.

P.J. Dunne gave me some old postcards together with books on the history of the postcard. I wish to thank him and Deirdre O'Connell who advised me on the history of fashion in Ireland. My thanks to Brian Flynn for providing me with office space when I had no place to lay my laptop. I am also indebted to David H. Davison. He assisted me in getting a selection of the Duncan photographs published in *The face of time* in 1995 and he wrote an informative introduction for it. He has come to the rescue again by reading this work, correcting some errors and writing a foreword for it. My thanks to E.E. O'Donnell for listing his books of Frank Browne's photographs.

Finally thanks to my family and friends and the parishioners of Denn who had to put up with my distracted ways while this work was being done.

Foreword

Photography, in all its manifestations, from television to x-ray imaging, is so pervasive that the relevance of the medium itself is frequently overlooked. Seldom do people pause to consider the motivation or vision within the mind of creators of these images. Film, whether documentary or dramatic, is usually the result of a collaborative team but is nonetheless directed by one creative mind.

Liam Kelly is right to emphasize the significance of the photographer's function when studying still photographs. Such stills are normally the product of one person and that individual's motives are, in themselves, of relevance. Photographs can be a means of record, but, who selects the content of that record? The very process of making a photograph involves interpretation and is amenable to control by the photographer who will formulate the image to express either his own or his client's concept or message. These latter aspects of the process will be influenced by the period and society within which the photographer operates. It is therefore always wise to ask when and why did the photographer make the image before interpreting its content.

It is refreshing to read an innovative work such as this, which highlights the fact that photographs represent an immensely rich and as yet largely untapped resource for historians who have tended to overlook photographs for purposes other than prettification. This book aims to rectify this imbalance of understanding. In a generation so accustomed to receiving information in visual format, it is timely that we consider the means of interpreting such material in detail. Liam Kelly is to be congratulated for providing a key with which a treasure chest of material, as yet unknown, can be opened.

David H. Davison
December 2007

Introduction

It is generally accepted that photography began in the year 1839. There had been attempts to create photographic images before that, but with Daguerre and Fox Talbot both publicizing their inventions within a short time of each other in middle of 1839, historians usually point to that period as the one in which photography began. The camera, more than most of the gadgets and machines developed during the so-called Industrial Revolution, would have a lasting and revolutionary effect on society, helping to create, in time, the visual and image-driven world we now live in.

It is difficult to overstate the impact early photographs had on those who saw them or even on those who heard about them. Being able to look at one's 'likeness' or a photograph of a familiar streetscape or landscape, forced people to look at the world in a new way and to ask basic questions about themselves and their world. It also forced them to ask questions about the nature and function of photography, a debate which is still on-going.

Once invented, interest in the camera and the photograph never waned even though the camera and the purposes it was used for changed with time. Some photographers tried to imitate art and others to create visual records of historic sites or artefacts. Photography was mostly restricted to the elite in society. It was used to create prison records and to aid police in their investigations, to document wars and poverty, to create pornography, to sell portraits or postcards, to advertize, to canvass votes at election time and for propaganda purposes. It was used to record events, to convey news and to sell newspapers. It was used to convey truth and to tell lies. In the recently published book *The genius of photography: how photography has changed our lives* (London, 2007) its author Gerry Badger writes:

> The photographic medium has such a diversity of aims and ambitions that to talk about a single unified story of photography is a nonsense. There are a number of stories of photography …[1]

The types of camera, people's understanding of photography and the uses it was put to have been evolving ever since 1839 and will continue to do so. Despite this change and diversity we need to write about photography if for no other reason than to try to understand it.

Historians have been slow to recognize photographs as useful primary sources in their research. They have tip-toed around the vast range of photographic documents created since 1839, only occasionally plucking one out and then using

---

1 Gerry Badger, *The genius of photography: how photography has changed our lives* (London, 2007), p. 7.

13

it merely for decorative purposes. It is true that not all photographs will yield evidence or information useful to the researcher – but one can say the same about manuscript documents or any other type of primary source. Photographs are important historical documents and useful primary sources for historical research. They are best used in conjunction with other primary sources. It is only in recent years that historians are beginning to give them the attention they deserve.

The definitive history of photography in Ireland has yet to be written. This short book does not attempt to do so. Rather it is meant to be a guide for researchers, giving them the basic information necessary to discover and decipher photographs. This book focuses mostly, though not entirely, on the nineteenth century when the camera and photographic processes were changing by the decade. Documentary photographers receive more attention in this book than other photographers since their images are more likely to yield evidence and information useful to the historian. The history of art photography in Ireland is not dealt with in this guide.

Chapter one gives a brief account of how the camera evolved in Europe and north America, providing a context and background against which the development of photography in Ireland can be understood. The second chapter deals briefly with the growth of photography in Ireland and identifies particularly significant photographers who influenced that growth. The third chapter lists some of the more important photographic collections, where they are held and how they can be accessed. Chapter four suggests a methodical approach to reading photographs and extracting reliable information from them. The fifth chapter highlights some of the advantages and pitfalls of historians using photographic evidence as primary sources. This chapter also gives practical advice to historians about discovering and handling old photographs.

Reading photographs or other visual images is a skill many historians believe they do not have. Photographs, when studied thoroughly and systematically, will often yield evidence and information which is not obvious at first glance and yet will prove invaluable to the historian. Photographic documents need to be studied by historians if for no other reason than they exist. It is hoped that this guide will encourage historians researching periods from the mid-nineteenth century onwards to include photographs among their primary sources.

CHAPTER I

A brief history of photography

THE EARLY YEARS

Human beings have always been interested in creating graphic visual representations of themselves and their surroundings. The cave art of primitive cultures and the high art of the Renaissance period attest to this. Mostly the visual representations were created by people co-ordinating hand and eye and using simple tools such as brush and paint, hammer and chisel. However, more sophisticated tools were also used to aid them in their work. As early as the fourth century BC Aristotle referred to an optical device – a box or darkened room with a small aperture on one side through which light shone and reflected an external image upside down on the opposite side – which artists could then use as an aid to drawing.[1] It was the German astronomer and mathematician, Johannes Kepler (1541–1630), who first called this device a 'camera obscura'.[2] Another gadget, the 'camera lucida'[3] – an artist's aid comprising lens and prism through which a virtual image is seen – was invented in 1674, though only patented by William Hyde Wollaston in 1806. These two 'drawing machines'[4], which used natural light to project an image onto a flat surface, were the forerunners of what we now call the camera.

The Englishman William Henry Fox Talbot (1800–77) was a renaissance man of sorts. An MP with a country estate at Lacock Abbey, he was also a classical scholar and scientist with a special interest in botany, chemistry and optics. He brought a camera lucida with him when he travelled to Italy in 1833 with his wife Constance and his mother Elizabeth and used it to make sketches in the Lake Como district. His sketches disappointed him greatly and he contrasted them with the rich images which he remembered a camera obscura could project. He wrote:

> And this led me to reflect on the inimitable beauty of the pictures of nature's painting which the glass lens of the camera throws upon the paper in its focus – fairy pictures, creations of moment and destined as rapidly to fade away.
>
> It was during these thoughts that the idea occurred to me … how charming it would be if it were possible to cause these natural images to

1 Michael Frizot (ed.), *The new history of photography* (English edition, Paris, 1998), p. 18. For a concise account of the early years of photography see Beaumont Newhall, *Photography: a short critical history* (New York, 1938), pp 11–18.   2 The Latin for a 'dark room'.   3 The Latin for a 'lighted room'.   4 This term was used by Michael Frizot. See *The new history of photography*, p. 17. William Henry Fox Talbot regarded photography as 'mechanised drawing'. See Estelle Jussim, *The eternal moment: essays on the photographic image* (New York, 1989), p. 12.

imprint themselves durably and remain fixed upon the paper! And why should it not be possible? I asked myself.[5]

The challenge was to capture and keep the image projected by the camera obscura. The solution would involve the sciences optics and chemistry. Several scientists, especially from 1800 onwards, were pre-occupied with this challenge and were experimenting with a variety of chemicals and lenses to find a method to create and chemically fix images produced by the light of the sun. The most notable of these scientists were Joseph N. Niépce, Louis M. Daguerre and Hippolyte Bayard in France. Thomas Wedgewood and W.H.F. Talbot were the best known figures in England. The work of these men is best understood against the background of the Industrial Revolution which was in full swing in the early decades of the 1800s. It was a time of experimentation and change with new inventions and new machines emerging with great regularity. The camera, which could create fixed images called photographs, was just another of these new machines. The historian John Tagg saw the camera as the product of an emerging middle class. He wrote:

> The incentive to develop the existing scientific and technical knowledge as a means of fixing the image of the camera obscura came ... from the unprece-dented demand for images among the newly dominant middle classes, at a stage of economic growth in Britain and France when organised industry was displacing traditional patterns of manufacture and laying the basis for a new social order.[6]

Daguerre and Niépce worked together in France on methods of fixing images until Niépce's death in 1833 after which Daguerre continued to work on his own. By 1839 he had developed a method of capturing and fixing an image and on 19 August of that year his invention was unveiled in the Institut de France and the birth of photography was announced to the world. Six months earlier, on 31 January, W.H.F. Talbot, spurred on by the news of Daguerre's progress in France, had a paper read to the Royal Society in London outlining his experiments and discoveries in photogenic drawing. He followed up this paper with a series of exhibitions to substantiate his claims. Both men were purporting to be the inventors of photography even though Hippoloyte Bayard (1801–87) had held an exhibition of his photographs on 24 June 1839. Both Daguerre and Talbot developed different types of primitive camera and varied methods of fixing their images. It is now generally accepted that they were the key figures in the birth of photography.[7]

5 William Henry Fox Talbot, 'Brief historical sketches of the invention of the art' in *The pencil of nature* (London, 1844), p. 1.   **6** John Tagg, *The burden of representation: essays on photographies and histories* (London, 1988), pp 40–1.   **7** Estelle Jussim considers Talbot to be the most important camera inventor at this time. She wrote: '... it is Talbot who is considered the Father of Modern Photography and the only philosophical genius among the gaggle of inventors who followed him'. Jussim, *The eternal moment*, p. 17. Alan Trachtenberg queries 1839 as the date of the birth of photography. He wrote 'With its

DAGUERREOTYPE AND CALOTYPE

Daguerre's method of photography became known as the 'daguerreotype.' It created a positive image on a sheet of copper which was plated with a thin coat of silver. It had to be exposed to the light for a period of ten to twenty minutes and was then developed over heated mercury. It was fixed with a solution of common salt and finally rinsed in warm distilled water. This laborious process, when carried out correctly, resulted in very accurate and detailed images. With more experimentation the exposure time was shortened to a period of between ten and thirty seconds. Daguerreotype studios sprang up during the 1840s in cities throughout Europe and the United States and those who could afford it queued to have their portraits taken. The best of the early photographs were Daguerreotype ones. However, the process had a number of drawbacks which eventually led to its demise. The method was difficult and dangerous since the individual who developed the pictures was exposed to toxic mercury fumes. It was also expensive. However, its greatest weakness was that it created only a single right to left image which could not be copied. Daguerreotype photography gradually disappeared during the 1850s when it was replaced by the wet collodion, negative/positive method of photography.

Between the years 1839 and 1841 Talbot, with the help of others, developed the 'calotype'[8] process of photography, which he duly patented in 1841. Unlike the Daguerreotype, which developed a positive print on a copper sheet, Talbot's method developed a latent negative print on paper which had been sensitized with a solution of silver nitrate and potassium iodide. The invisible image was then developed with a solution of gallo-nitrate of silver in a darkened room. Exposure time for calotype negatives was several minutes, depending on the light. The calotype negatives were generally not as clear as the Daguerreotype ones. However, their main advantage was that the negatives produced by this method could generate many copies of the image. Talbot's *The pencil of nature*, published in six parts between 1844 and 1846, was the first book to be published with photographic illustrations. In the mid-1840s Talbot set up a photographic printing and developing facility at Reading. At the time of his death in 1877 it was obvious that subsequent developments in photography would be based on the negative/positive method he had pioneered.[9]

official appearance in 1839 (the first known photograph was made about a dozen years earlier)'. See Alan Trachtenberg (ed.), *Classic essays on photography* (New York, 1980), p. xii. Geoffrey Batchen, in his book *Burning with desire, the conception of photography* (Boston, 1997) claims that others, in such diverse countries as the United States, Switzerland, Spain and Brazil, were experimenting with primitive cameras before 1839. See pp 24–53.   **8** It was sometimes referred to as the 'Talbotype' process. Calotype took its name from the Greek words 'kalos' – meaning 'beautiful' and 'typus' meaning 'image'. Talbot saw photography as an artistic endeavour.   **9** Some of Talbot's prints, negatives, note-books and cameras are in the National Museum of Photography, Film and Television in Bradford. For an introduction to his life and for some of his best early prints see A. Burnett-Brown, M. Gray & R. Roberts

WET COLLODION PROCESS

The two methods of photography which existed in the 1840s were slow and cumbersome, difficult and expensive. Inevitably photographers were looking for better and easier ways to take photographs. Frederick Scott Archer (1813–57) worked in London as a sculptor and from 1847 onwards was using calotype photography to help him in his work. He was dissatisfied with the uneven surface of the paper negatives and he experimented with various solutions and surfaces in an attempt to improve the process. In March 1851 he announced a new method which involved coating a glass plate with a sensitized collodion solution, exposing it and developing it while still wet.[10] The results were very impressive. This method gave a sharp clear image like the Daguerreotype and it could be easily copied like the calotype. Moreover, it reduced the exposure time and in doing so increased the range of photography.

Glass negatives produced by the wet collodion method were then converted into positive paper prints. At first the salted paper, favoured by Talbot, was used with some success. In 1850 the French photographer Louis Désiré Blanquart-Evrard (1802–72), building on the earlier work of Talbot, discovered that the white of an egg, when beaten to a foam and spread evenly onto paper, proved an excellent sealer and adhesive base onto which silver nitrate could then be applied. Very quickly albumen paper became the preferred printing paper of photography and from 1860 until the mid-1880s it was used almost exclusively by photographers. Commercially prepared albumen paper was available from 1855 onwards, the largest factory being in the German city of Dresden. Gradually, from the mid-1880s, the use of albumen paper was on the wane, though some photographers continued to use it into the twentieth century.[11]

The wet collodion method of photography did not always lead to albumen paper prints. The ambrotype method, which placed an under-exposed glass plate negative against a dark background to give a positive image, was developed by Frederick Scott Archer and Peter Fry in the early 1850s and patented by James Ambrose Cutting in 1854. The dark background was achieved by painting the underside of the glass with black paint or by placing the glass plate against a background of dark cloth, metal or paper and securing it in a frame or case. The image produced by this method was usually black and grey[12], and like the Daguerreotype, the ambrotype created a single image which was reversed right to left. The ambrotype method was used mostly in the period 1853 to 1865. It was popular for a time because it was relatively cheap, though the long exposure time needed and the fragility of the glass plate were disadvantages that gradually lead to

(eds), *Specimens and marvels: William Henry Fox Talbot and the invention of photography* (Bradford, 2000). This book was published by the Aperture Foundation to mark the bicentenary of Talbot's birth.   **10** Frederick Scott Archer, 'On the use of collodion in photography' in *The Chemist*, 2 (Mar. 1851), p. 257.   **11** See article by James M. Reilly, 'The history, technique and structure of albumen prints' (http://albumen.stanford.edu/library/ c20reilly1980.html) (12 Feb. 2007).   **12** Some had colour added later by hand painting.

it being replaced by other methods. Tintype photography, which evolved from the ambrotype method, was invented by Hamilton L. Smith (1819–1903) in Ohio in 1856. Tintype photographs (also known as ferrotype or melainotype) were negatives on a thin piece of black enamelled or japanned iron. Both ambrotype and tintype photography were created by a collodion negative appearing as a positive when placed against a dark background. Both processes resulted in a reversed left to right image. The tintype method had several advantages over the ambrotype and so it endured for a much longer period. It produced a cheap image very quickly. The light metal-based image was more robust and durable than the ambrotype one and tintype photography became especially popular during the American Civil War when soldiers could safely post their photographs home to their loved ones. Studios seldom used the tintype method because the resulting photograph sometimes lacked clarity. It was a method preferred by itinerant street and beach photographers and it continued in use, in some instances, until the 1960s.

The wet collodion process, available from 1851 onwards, was an important breakthrough for photography. It became the standard method of photography for the next three decades and helped its rapid growth in those years. Despite the developments, photographers who used the wet collodion method had to have many skills. They had to be technically capable and physically strong to manage the large camera, clumsy tripod, portable darkroom, glass plates, chemicals and water, dishes and tank required for the procedure. They had to be scientists of sorts to know how to treat the glass plates and to develop the negatives on location. They had to have the aesthetic sense and sharp eye that all good photographers need and they had to have a strong personality to engage their subjects and keep them from moving during the still relatively long exposure time. The studio photographer had an easier task than his travelling counterpart. Because of the amount of equipment needed to take a photograph, travelling photographers could not stray far from some mode of transport, though they were fortunate that the rail systems were growing at the same time as photography.

The real boom in photography did not happen until the 1860s. It was, before that time, relatively expensive to have one's portrait taken in a photographic studio. By the 1860s that had changed, largely due to the work of the French photographer Andre Adolphe Disdéri (1819–90). In 1854 Disdéri patented *carte-de-visite* photography. He showed how, with the use of a sliding plate holder and a camera with four lenses, eight negatives could be taken on a single 8" x 10" glass plate. The positive image from this process was 2½" x 4". The *carte-de-visite* photograph became very popular because its small size meant that it could be sent in the post or kept in an album or even in a coat pocket. By 1859 the *carte-de-visite* style portraits were in vogue in New York. Jane Welsh Carlyle remarked in that same year 'this art [photography] by which even the poor can possess themselves of tolerable likenesses of their absent dear ones'.[13] Soon it became more fashionable for

13 Quoted in Allan Sekula, 'The body and the archive' in Richard Bolton (ed.), *The contest of meaning, critical histories of photography* (Boston, 1992), p. 346.

American Civil War soldiers to bring a *carte-de-visite* rather than a tintype of their loved ones into battle with them. It was much cheaper to produce than the earlier method of having a single image on the large glass plate. 'With the *carte-de-visite*, photography slid out of frames on the wall and into albums on the table.'[14]

The cumbersome camera and the long exposure time associated with photography during the first decades meant that many of the early outdoor pictures were static ones showing landscape, antiquities, architecture or other inanimate objects. Despite many difficulties some photographers did attempt documentary photography in this early period. Herman Biow (1804–50) took Daguerreotype pictures of the devastation caused by the great Hamburg fire in May 1842. Roger Fenton (1819–69) was commissioned by the British government in 1855 to photograph the Crimean War. He and his assistants took more than 350 photographs; however, his pictures are peripheral shots and give a very sanitised view of the war:

> Fenton's war pictures … tend to portray war as a gorgeous pageant. There are
> no dead bodies, and one might almost imagine that the Crimean War was
> almost like a picnic. There are no action shots (this for technical reasons), but
> those of soldiers are carefully posed groups, almost as if they were cricketers
> just about to go in to bat … moreover as an agent of the government his
> portrayals were somewhat slanted.[15]

The American photographer Matthew Brady (1823–96)[16] and his team took approximately 8,000 pictures during the American Civil War (1861–5). They were usually taken either before or after the fighting, though in some instances their pictures do show dead bodies and capture some of the harsh reality of war.

Photographs, especially in the decade after 1839, caused quite a stir. Those who saw them marvelled at them and were curious about the process that created them. Despite the scientific age some thought photographs were created through supernatural or preternatural intervention. W.H.F. Talbot's notebooks and letters are speckled with such phrases as 'fairy pictures,' 'the black art' and 'magic pictures' to describe the new phenomenon. Talbot's friend, John Herschel, jokingly accused him: 'surely you deal with the naughty one'.[17] Despite the great curiosity photography generated, it was at first practised only by the privileged few who had the money and the skills to do so. Photographic societies, exhibitions, journals and competitions all helped the spread of photography and fostered the debate about its nature and function.[18] The Société Héliographique, set up in France in 1851, launched their journal *La Lumiére* in the same year that photographs from Britain, France and the United States were on show at the Great Exhibition held in the

14 Jean Sagne, 'All kinds of portraits' in Frizot (ed.), *The new history of photography*, p. 110. **15** Robert Leggat, 'A history of photography' (http://www.rleggat.com/photohistory/ history/fenton.htm) (21 Oct. 2006).   **16** He was born in Warren County in New York state to Irish immigrant parents.   **17** These quotes are cited in Burnett-Brown, Gray & Roberts (eds), *Specimens and marvels*, pp 9–10. See also footnote 10.   **18** One of the main debates of this period was the connection between art, science and photography.

Crystal Palace.[19] In 1852 the first exhibition comprising only photographs was organized by the Royal Society of Art in London. In January 1853 the Photographic Society of London, which later became the Royal Photographic Society, was set up. The first issue of *The Royal Photographic Society Journal* stated that:

> The object of the Photographic Society is the promotion of the Art and Science of photography, by the interchange of thought and experience among photographers, and it is hoped that this object may, to some considerable extent, be effected by the periodical meetings of the society.[20]

GELATIN DRY PLATE PROCESS

Photography continued to gain popularity in the 1850s and 1860s despite the fact that the wet plate collodion process was a messy one and required a portable darkroom in order to develop the pictures on location. During the 1870s attempts were made to find a dry plate method of photography to replace it. In 1871 Richard L. Maddox, a London physician, suggested that plates could be prepared in advance by mixing a warm solution of gelatine with calcium bromide and silver nitrate, spreading them on a glass plate and allowing them to dry.[21] These early gelatin dry plates required longer exposure time than the wet plates and were no great advantage.[22] However, by 1878 Charles Bennet had improved the dry plate process and thus revolutionized photography.[23] This new development meant that dry plates could now be prepared in advance and within a short period several companies were manufacturing them. The exposure time was shortened to less than a second and the two processes of taking a picture and developing it were now separated. Developing could now be carried out at a later time and place that suited the photographer.

The task of taking a photograph became much simpler and faster and the photographer no longer had to haul around the various chemicals and the portable dark room. The photographer's kit now consisted of camera, tripod and a box of prepared dry plates. Because of the fast exposure time there was now less need for the tripod to steady the camera and gradually photographers began to dispense with it and use hand-held cameras instead. George Eastman, an American bank clerk with an interest in photography, read about Charles Bennet's dry-plate method and in 1881 set up the Eastman Dry Plate Company in Rochester which

19 See 'Introduction' in Mark Harworth-Booth, *The origins of British photography* (London, 1991). **20** *Royal Photographic Society Journal*, 3 Mar. 1853; Robert Leggat, 'The origins of the Royal Photographic Society' (http://www.rleggat.com/photohistory/royal_ph.htm) (20 Oct. 2006). **21** *British Journal of Photography*, 18 Sept. 1871; Jean-Claud Gautrand, 'Photography on the spur of the moment' in Frizot (ed.), *The new history of photography*, p. 233. **22** Brian Coe, *The birth of photography, the story of the formative years, 1800–1900* (London, 1976), p. 39. **23** *British Journal of Photography*, 29 Mar. 1878.

manufactured and sold dry plates on a commercial scale. Eastman realized that the glass plates needed for photography were heavy, fragile and expensive and so he experimented with dry coated paper and later with celluloid film on a spool. In 1888 his company began to manufacture the 'Kodak' camera and promoted it with the slogan 'you press the button, we do the rest'.[24] When the roll of sensitized paper was used, the camera was sent back to the factory to have it removed, developed and the camera re-loaded with a new roll before it was returned to its owner, ready for use again.

By 1890 photography had become a process which virtually anyone could manage. The small hand-held camera with the split-second exposure time increased greatly the range of photographs which could be taken. Since 1839 the camera had been refined and simplified through several stages. In 1860 John Herschel was so excited by the short exposure time of the wet collodion process that he coined the phrase 'snapshot' to describe what was then thought to be an instantaneous photograph.[25] Though his use of the term was somewhat premature, it has nonetheless survived. It was only in the 1880s, with the advent of the dry plate method and the Kodak camera, that a photograph could accurately be described as a 'snapshot.'

Roger Fenton and his team were criticized for mixing mainly with the officer classes during the Crimean War and including them in most of their pictures. They should not be criticized too much because for the first four decades after the camera was invented photography was, by and large, for the wealthier classes. Only they had the money and the time to learn the difficult techniques involved in taking a photograph and only they could afford to pay to have their pictures taken. In general, during this period, the poor and the socially deprived were excluded from photographs. There were exceptions, however. Thomas Annan (1829–87) photographed the slums of Glasgow between the years 1868 and 1877.[26] John Thomson (1837–1921) took pictures of street life in London in the 1870s and in the early years of the twentieth century Eugene Atget (1856–1927) took great shots of all aspects of Paris life. Jacob Riis photographed the poverty of New York slums in the 1890s. Lewis Hine took photographs of immigrants at Ellis Island in 1905 and later he highlighted, with his camera, the impoverished conditions in the slums of Washington DC and in the industrialized city of Pittsburgh.[27] These were crusading photographers because their images highlighted not just the conditions the poor had to live in but also pleaded 'do something about it'. From the 1880s onwards photographs were used to highlight the great social inequalities that existed and from this period onwards they were less exclusive in the people and the situations they depicted.

24 For a good account of the development of the Kodak camera see Gautrand, 'Photography on the spur of the moment' in Frizot (ed.), *The new history of photography*, pp 237–9.   25 *The Photographic News*, 11 May 1860.   26 Thomas Annan, *Photographs of the old closes and streets of Glasgow, 1868–1877* (Glasgow, 1878); Anon., *The origins of British photography* (London, 1981) with an introduction by Mark Haworth-Booth, p. 34.   27 Lewis W. Hine, 'Social photography' in Alan Trachtenberg (ed.), *Classic essays on photography* (New Haven, CT, 1980), pp 109–13.

The new types of cameras which emerged during the 1880s were much more suitable than earlier models for documentary photography and photo-journalism. Now there was less need to stage a picture in order to get a good photograph. However, newspapers were slow to use photographic illustrations and they were not able to adopt photography for use with columns of type until the end of the nineteenth century. Even in the first decade of the twentieth century newspapers used photographs sparingly because of the difficulties involved and because very often by the time photographs reached the editor's desk they were already several days out of date. It was not until after the First World War that photographs became commonplace in newspapers and from then on some newspapers began to build up good photographic collections which are now useful to historians.

FLASH BULBS AND COLOUR PHOTOGRAPHY

Indoor photography was still a problem in the 1880s because of the lack of light. To counteract this problem a method of creating artificial light using magnesium flash powder was invented in 1887. It was not until the 1930s that the dangerous flash powder was gradually replaced by flash bulbs developed at the Massachusetts Institute of Technology. Like the early camera, the first flashbulbs were large, expensive and cumbersome. Gradually they were refined and reduced in size so that they could be built into a pocket camera.

All the early methods of photography reduced a multicoloured world to black-and-white images. Some early photographs, especially Daguerreotypes, were later hand-painted by artists in an attempt to mimic the original colours. In 1859 James C. Maxwell, a Scottish physicist, demonstrated that all colours could be reduced to three primary colours – red, blue and green. This was an important breakthrough and many attempts were made to apply it to photography. Thomas Sutton (1819–75), who set up a photographic studio in Jersey in 1855, provided some of the practical skills to put Maxwell's theories into practice. It was not until 1907 that the big breakthrough came when the French brothers Auguste and Louis Lumiere developed the auto chrome glass. In the 1890s John Joly (1857–1933), a lecturer in the Physics Department in Trinity College Dublin, experimented quite successfully with colour photography. However, the definition and colour of the pictures still left much to be desired and it was not until 1935 that the first modern Kodachrome camera was introduced.[28] Instant photography was invented by the American Edwin H. Land, who developed the Polaroid camera in 1947 and a colour version came on the market in 1963. With the advent of the Polaroid camera, the two process of photographing and developing were once more brought together. The photographer pressed the button, the camera did the rest.

28 Jack Coote, *The illustrated history of colour photography* (London, 1993).

THE DIGITAL REVOLUTION

W.H.F. Talbot's negative/positive process which he developed in the years 1839–41 and George Eastman's introduction of celluloid film rolls in the 1880s were the basic techniques still used in most cameras one hundred years later. The methods they devised were refined, improved and built on. In general cameras became smaller, cheaper and easier to use, while the number of cameras and photographs taken continued to increase. In the last decades of the twentieth century the development of digital technology revolutionized photography. The technology needed for digital or film-less photography, which uses electrical devices to record imagery, was developed over a number of decades. In 1969 the Americans George Smith and William Boyle invented the charge-coupled device – the image sensor that is now used in digital cameras. Further developments were relatively slow. It was not until 1981 that Sony produced their magnetic video camera called 'Mavica' and the first digital camera for general use was the 'Apple Quick 100' which went on the marked in 1994. In 1995 when Kodak launched their 'Kodak DC40' the digital revolution was truly underway. Sales of digital cameras now surpass those of the traditional type of camera.

With the arrival of the miniature pocket-sized digital camera photography has come a long way from the large and unwieldy wooden cameras of the late 1830s. The methods of creating photographic images then and now are worlds apart.

CHAPTER 2

The growth of photography in Ireland

THE EARLY YEARS

There was widespread poverty and the looming catastrophe of famine in Ireland in the late 1830s when Talbot and Daguerre were announcing their inventions and showing their cameras and fixed images to the world. Despite the unfavourable conditions for the growth in photography in Ireland it was practised by some individuals in Belfast and Dublin very soon after it had begun in England and France.

On 20 September 1839 Francis Stewart Beatty, an engraver who lived at Castle Street in Belfast, wrote to the *Belfast Newsletter* claiming that he had succeeded in making negatives in the Daguerreotype fashion and he enclosed some samples of his work as evidence when writing to the editor.[1] Despite this early foray into camera work, photography was slow to take hold in Ireland. Instruction in the use of the Daguerreotype camera was given at the Dublin Mechanics Institute in Lower Abbey Street from 1840 onwards. In October 1841 the first commercial Daguerreotype studio was set up at the Rotunda in Dublin. An advertisement in the *Freeman's Journal*, dated 16 October 1841, publicised the new studio and was addressed to 'the Nobility, Gentry and citizens of Dublin', though it was only the first two categories mentioned who could hope to avail of it since it cost £1 1s. to have a portrait taken.[2] Several other Daguerreotype studios were set up during the 1840s in Dublin along a line from St Stephen's Green to the top of Sackville Street.[3] Most of the Daguerreotype studios in Ireland were situated in either Dublin or Belfast, though some Daguerreotype photographers travelled to provincial towns to take photographs.[4]

The new photographic studios which sprung up in Dublin and elsewhere in the 1840s allowed people who could not afford to have an artist paint their portrait to

---

1 Reprinted in Edward Chandler, *Photography in Ireland: the nineteenth century* (Dublin, 2001), p. 5. For more information on Beatty see W.A. Maguire, *A century in focus: photography and photographers in the north of Ireland, 1839–1939* (Belfast, 2000), pp 2–7. **2** Chandler, *Photography in Ireland: the nineteenth century*, p. 15. **3** For a good account of the turf war between these photographers see Chandler, *Photography in Ireland: the nineteenth century*, pp 13–28. **4** The higher density of professional photographers on the east coast of Ireland, especially in Dublin and Belfast, continued throughout the nineteenth century. There were 52 professional photographers based in Dublin city in 1861, 9 in Belfast and only 41 in the rest of the country. See Peadar Slattery, 'The uses of photography in Ireland, 1839–1900' (2 vols, PhD thesis, Trinity College, Dublin, 1991), ii, Appendix B, pp 144–5.

2.1 One of the oldest surviving photographs taken in Ireland. Nelson's pillar and Sackville Street, *c.*1845 (courtesy of Irish Picture Library)

procure a portrait by a quicker and cheaper method. The inability to copy Daguerreotype pictures was a major drawback. Artists such as Henry O'Neill helped to overcome the problem by making remarkably accurate lithographic copies of some of them, which in turn could be copied as often as was required. A Daguerreotype photograph of Daniel O'Connell was taken, probably while he was in jail in 1844, and although the original photograph has not survived, the lithographic copy has.[5] Other artists hand painted some of the Daguerreotype photographs in an attempt to mimic the original colour.[6]

5 Chandler, *Photography in Ireland: the nineteenth century*, p. 22.   6 For examples of hand-painted Irish portraits which were taken in the 1850s see Seán Sexton & Christine Kinealy, *The Irish: a photohistory* (London, 2002), pp 12–13.

William Parsons, third earl of Rosse, began experimenting with the Daguerreotype processes in June 1842 at his home in Birr Castle, Co. Offaly. None of his photographs from this period have survived. In 1852 he exchanged letters with W.H.F. Talbot and by the following year his wife, Mary, countess of Rosse, was praised by Talbot for the quality of her photography.[7] Leone Glukman, who had his studio at 13 Lower Sackville Street, was one of the most colourful of the early Daguerreotype photographers in Dublin. He photographed some of the leading figures in Ireland during the 1840s, including the Young Ireland leaders Thomas Davis, Thomas Francis Meagher and William Smith O'Brien. Photographs of Davis and Meagher have survived as has a lithographic copy of O'Brien. However, very few Daguerreotype photographs have survived from this period.

It was not W.H.F. Talbot's workshop at Reading but rather St Andrew's College in Edinburgh, which was outside the control of Talbot's patent restrictions, that became the most influential centre in the promotion of the calotype photographs in Ireland during the 1840s. In general the daguerreotype photography was practised by professionals operating out of studios while the calotype was operated, mostly outdoors, by gifted amateurs who were wealthy and skilled enough to do so. Two Irishmen, William Holland Furlong who worked in the chemistry department at St Andrew's, and Michael Packenham Edgeworth, half-brother of the novelist Maria Edgeworth, were calotype photographers and part of the St Andrew's circle. A small number of Furlong's pictures have survived and can be found in the J. Paul Getty Museum in Los Angeles and in the Scottish National Portrait Gallery in Edinburgh. Some of Edgeworth's photographs are also housed in the Getty Museum as are images taken at Buttevant in Co. Cork in 1842 by Henry Brewster.[8]

William Despard Hemphill, who would later become one of the most important nineteenth-century Irish photographers, was studying medicine in St Andrew's in the early 1840s, and while there became interested in the new phenomena of photography. Later, when practising as a medical doctor in Co. Tipperary, he would put his camera skills to good use.[9] Patrick Byrne, the blind Irish harpist, visited Edinburgh in 1844 where he had his photograph taken.[10] A small number of Dublin streetscape photographs from the mid-1840s have survived and are part of the Fox Talbot Collection in the National Museum of Photography, Film & Television in Bradford.

The daguerreotype and calotype methods of photography which were available in the 1840s were so difficult to execute and so expensive to operate that relatively few photographs were taken in Ireland in this period and even fewer have survived.

7 David H. Davison, *Impressions of an Irish Countess: the photography of Mary, countess of Rosse* (Birr, 1989), p. 3. 8 Chandler, *Photography in Ireland: the nineteenth century*, pp 8–9. 9 W.D. Hemphill's earliest surviving photograph was taken in 1853. The calotype method had been replaced by the wet collodion method by then. For information on Hemphill's photography see Pat Holland, *Tipperary images: the photography of Dr William Despard Hemphill* (Cahir, 2003). 10 Chandler, *Photography in Ireland: the nineteenth century*, plate 5.

The daguerreotype camera often produced good results in a studio setting, though these studios were limited mostly to the cities and to the larger provincial towns. The primitive cameras of the 1840s were not suitable for photojournalism and consequently we have no images depicting the Great Irish Famine of the late 1840s, even though the camera had been invented almost a decade earlier.

PIONEER PHOTOGRAPHERS

John Shaw Smith (1811–73), the son of a Co. Cork landlord, took many photographs during the late 1840s and early 1850s.[11] Approximately 360 of his calotype negatives have survived from this period and they are to be found in the George Eastman House at Rochester in New York. Most of his pictures were taken while travelling in France, Italy, Greece and Egypt, though 15 of the surviving pictures were taken in Ireland. The Irish pictures are mostly of Glendalough, Powerscourt, and the high crosses at Monasterboice and Rostrevor. British amateur photographers travelled to Ireland in the 1850s and took photographs, mainly of scenic views, which they later exhibited in London. In 1854 Alfred Rosling exhibited 'The Gap of Dunlow' and 'Muckross Abbey' while Peter Wickens Fry exhibited 'Glenade, County Leitrim' at Royal Society of Arts.[12]

The estate papers of the landed gentry, in many instances, include photographs. A good example is the collection of Annesley papers relating to the family's estate at Castlewellan in Co. Down, which are to be found in the Public Records Office of Northern Ireland.[13] Hugh, fifth earl of Annesley, was a soldier[14], diarist and amateur photographer. He fought in the Kaffir War in South Africa and in the Crimean War and took photographs of these places and elsewhere. He also took many Irish photographs on his estate and other views around Castlewellan, Donard Lodge, Newcastle and the Mourne mountains. There are 35 albums of photographs in the Annesley papers. This photographic collection covers a forty-year period, starting in 1855, and is the largest and most important early photographic collection in the north-east of the country.

Edward King Tenison and his wife Louisa, who lived at Kilronan Castle in Co. Roscommon, acquired a licence from W.H.F. Talbot in the early 1850s to use his calotype method. They took photographs mostly of the built environment, the big houses and churches in Roscommon and the neighbouring counties of Mayo and Longford. The positive images were kept in an album, now called the 'Kilronan album' and 106 of them are to be found in the Irish National Photographic Archive

11 Slattery, 'The uses of photography in Ireland, 1839–1900', i, 178–9.   12 Ibid., ii, 126. 13 There are also photographs in the Lisadell papers in PRONI. These photographs are mostly of big houses and their occupants. There are photographs in this collection of places as far apart as Adare Manor in Limerick and Crom Castle in Fermanagh.   14 Henry Brewster who took the early photographs at Buttevant, was also a soldier. Taking photographs was a hobby for quite a few military people and their different postings enabled

Feb. 20 /64

2.2 Lady Augusta Crofton Dillon took this photograph of Lord Dunlo and the Dillon sisters with a stereo camera at Clonbrock House Co. Galway on 20 February 1864 (CLON 488)[15] (courtesy of National Photographic Archive)

in Temple Bar, Dublin.[16] More of the King Tenison photographs are to be found in the Irish Picture Library.[17] The King Tenison photographs are important images of the north-west of Ireland in the early decades of photography, even if their range is limited.

The Dublin Photographic Society, which was set up in November 1854, helped promote photography in Dublin and even had its own journal for a short period.[18] Society members were predominantly wealthy gentlemen enthusiasts who had enough money and time to pursue their hobby of taking photographs. Mary, countess of Rosse, who joined the society in 1856, was soon winning prizes for her photography. Her best-surviving photographs were taken in the mid-1850s. Her pictures are mostly of her family and friends, of Birr Castle and town and of the large telescope, called 'the Leviathan', at Birr Castle. Her portraits are skilfully arranged and executed and have more life in them than most of the early photographs.[19]

them to document their travels. 15 Note the date the photograph was taken is written on the bottom right hand corner of the image. 16 Sarah Rouse, *Into the light: an illustrated guide to the photographic collections in the National Library of Ireland* (Dublin, 1998), pp 52–3. 17 The Irish Picture Library, 69B Heather Road, Sandyford Industrial estate, Dublin 18. 18 Chandler, *Photography in Ireland: the nineteenth century*, pp 65–70. The Belfast Photographic Society was set up in 1857. It only lasted for three years. See Maguire, *A century in focus*, p. 13. 19 For examples of her photography and an informative text see Davison, *Impressions of an Irish Countess*. Birr Castle photographic library contains many interesting books on the early

Another woman from the landed gentry class, Lady Augusta Crofton Dillon of Clonbrock in Galway, was also a skilled photographer and contributed greatly to the Clonbrock Photographic Collection which comprises 3,500 pictures taken between 1860 and 1930. This collection is now available for consultation in the National Photographic Archive in Temple Bar.[20] The early skilled amateur photographers in Ireland, both women and men, tended to come from the landed gentry class. They have created a large volume of photographic documentation which is useful to historians researching the landed gentry and big houses of nineteenth-century Ireland. The range of these photographs is limited, however, because such photographers seldom strayed with their cameras beyond their own circle of family and friends or indeed beyond their demesne walls.

William Despard Hemphill (1816–1902), a medical doctor based in Clonmel, Co. Tipperary, was a skilled photographer with a keen aesthetic sense. He took many photographs spanning much of the second half of the nineteenth century and most were taken in Clonmel and the surrounding area in south Tipperary and north Waterford. Some of his photographs, such as his 'summer fruit' taken in 1864 and his 'white currants' taken in 1867, are fine examples of early photography imitating art. W.D. Hemphill strived after beauty in his finely staged pictures and many of his photographs won prizes at exhibitions in Dublin, London and Paris. Among his photographs which are of greatest interest to historians are those of the built environment, life in the big house, and military personnel based in Clonmel. Pat Holland's *Tipperary images: the photographs of Dr William Despard Hemphill* details how the exposure time for his photographs varied greatly from as little as a few seconds to as much as thirty minutes. He is one of the most important and prolific of the early photographers in Ireland.[21]

Lady Clementina Hawarden (1822–65) also took excellent photographs in Co. Tipperary in the early decades of photography. She was born Clementina Elphinstone Fleming[22] and lived her early years in Scotland before marrying Cornwallis Maude. The couple lived in London and in 1856 Cornwallis Maude became Viscount Hawarden and inherited the large family estate at Dundrum in Co. Tipperary. They lived on the Dundrum estate from 1857 to 1859 when they returned to London. Lady Clementina regularly visited Dundrum until her untimely death in 1865. She took some excellent photographs on and near the Dundrum estate between 1857 and 1864. She had a keen artistic eye and while many of her photographs are dreamy and moody, there is much in them to interest the historian in these early years when the camera was still in its infancy. Her picture of the carpenter at his workbench, the fiddler and friends and the picture of the camera and tripod against

photographic processes.   **20** Rouse, *Into the light*, p. 15; Michael O'Connell, *Shadows: an album of the Irish people, 1841–1914* (Dublin, 1985), pp 28–39.   **21** Dr Hemphill published a book of photographs in 1860 titled *Stereoscopic illustrations of Clonmel and the surrounding country, including abbeys, castles and scenery with descriptive letterpress*. See also Holland, *Tipperary images*.   **22** Virginia Dodier, *Lady Clementina Hawarden: studies of life, 1857–1864* (London, 1999); Carol Mayor, *Becoming: the photographs of Clementina, Viscountess Hawarden* (London, 1999).

2.3 Photograph by Lady Clementina Hawarden of the carpenter in his workshop at Dundrum House, Co. Tipperary, *c*.1862 (courtesy of Victoria and Albert Museum)

the background of the East wing of Dundrum House are all excellent documentary-type photographs. Thanks to the camera work of two gifted photographers, Lady Hawarden and Dr Hemphill, Co. Tipperary has more surviving images from the early decades of photography than many counties in Ireland.

Alexander Ayton, a Scottish photographer, who set up a studio in Derry in the early 1860s, is best known for his much re-produced picture of people at an open air Mass in Donegal in 1867. However, he also took excellent photographs of the houses and people on Tory Island and the west coast of Donegal in the 1860s. The originals of these photographs have not survived, though some have been published in *Sights and scenes in Ireland* (London, 1898).[23] James Glass (1847–1931) was another photographer with a studio in Carlisle Road in Derry. He too took photographs in Co. Donegal. Twenty-four of his pictures, taken to document evictions in the Gweedore area of Donegal in the late 1880s, have survived.[24]

Sir Joscelyn Coghill (1826–1905), who lived at Drishane in Co. Cork, was a skilled photographer and was active in promoting photography in Ireland through his work in organizing photographic societies and exhibitions. He was secretary of the Dublin Photographic Society in the mid-1850s, and in 1857 he exhibited nine landscape photographs at the Manchester Art Treasures Exhibition. Coghill was director of the photographic section of the Dublin International Exhibition in 1865 and in that capacity he wrote to W.H.F. Talbot stating that 'all British photographers acknowledge [Talbot] as father of their art'[25] and outlining why he thought photography should be included under the heading 'Fine Arts' in the exhibition. Coghill showed twelve photographs at that exhibition which he had taken in the neighbourhood of Castletownshend, Co. Cork. Two years earlier he won a prize at an exhibition in Paris for his photograph of Roger's Island. While copies of 49 of his pictures are in the National Photographic Archives in Temple Bar,[26] more of his pictures are housed in the Getty Museum in Los Angeles and at the George Eastman House in Rochester, New York.

PRISONER PHOTOGRAPHY[27]

It was not just the privileged who were photographed at this time. Prisoners also had their pictures taken. In 1854 Sir Walter Crofton was appointed chairman of the newly established Convict Prisons Board in Ireland. He was intent on reforming the prisons and saw photography as an important element in the control and supervision of former convicts.[28] The practice of taking mug shots of convicts in Irish prisons began in 1857 and Frederick Holland Mares was the first photographer contracted for this purpose. The practice was well established by 1860 when the Prisons Board report of that year stated that 'photography assists identification

23 Maguire, *A century in focus*, pp 30–3.   **24** Ibid., pp 66–8.   **25** http://www.foxtalbot.arts. gla.ac.uk/corresp (13 Nov. 2006). The letter is dated 31 Dec. 1864.   **26** Rouse, *Into the light*, p. 17.   **27** Alphonse Bertillion, director of the identification bureau of the Paris Prefecture of Police, invented the first rigorous system of archival cataloguing and retrieval of photographs. His system quickly spread to other police forces. See A. Sekula, 'The body and the archive' in R. Bolton (ed.), *The contest of meaning: critical histories of photography*, pp 355–72. **28** Elizabeth Dooley, 'Sir Walter Crofton and the Irish intermediate system of prison discipline' in Ian McDonnell & Finbarr McCauley (eds), *Criminal justice history: themes and controversies from pre-independence Ireland* (Dublin, 2003); Slattery, 'The uses of photography in

and every male prisoner entering the Irish convict establishments has his photograph taken.'[29] Many of the prisoners were photographed as they left prison, though some of them had their pictures taken at three-year intervals during their stay in prison. The county jails were operated under a different system and its photographing of prisoners was more haphazard. It was not until 1869 that it was required by law that all prisoners have their photographs taken on entry into the prison system. These mug shots, showing a front and side view of each prisoner, are a good and reliable documentary source for historians.[30] Pictures and descriptions of prisoners from all over the country exist, especially for the period 1881–1927. These photographs are to be found in the penal records of the General Prisons Board, in the National Archives, Bishop's Street, Dublin.

Individual amateur enthusiasts and professional studio photographers helped the spread of photography in Ireland in the nineteenth century. The growth was patchy, however. Despite the growing popularity of photography in the country there were still no professional photographers in counties Carlow, Wicklow, Offaly or Sligo in 1871.[31] The development of the dry plate process in the late 1870s and the Kodak camera and celluloid film in the 1880s left photography easier and cheaper and speeded up the spread of photography in Ireland. Two family-owned and Dublin-based photographic studios, the Lafayette and Lawrence studios, contributed greatly to the growth of photography in Ireland in the last two decades of the nineteenth century.

LAFAYETTE AND LAWRENCE

The Lafayette studio was set up at 30 Westmoreland Street in 1880 by James Stack Lauder. He was the eldest son of Edmund Lauder who had a daguerreotype studio in the city as early as 1853 and he adopted the chic sounding French name 'Lafayette' to boost his business. This new venture flourished and soon became the leading portrait studio in Ireland, winning many medals for its photography. The business secured contracts to photograph Queen Victoria and other members of the royal family and in 1887 Lafayette's was given the title 'Her Majesty's photographer in Dublin'.[32] It was now a mark of success to have one's photograph taken by Lafayette. The business expanded rapidly with branches being set up in Glasgow (1890), Manchester (1892), London (1897) and Belfast (1900). The Lafayette studios amassed a large store of portrait negatives. Unfortunately most of the glass negative were destroyed in 1951. However, portraits of such eminent figures as Patrick Pearse, George Bernard Shaw and William B. Yeats have survived. Positive Lafayette images are to be found in many private houses and local library collections and are easily identifiable by the distinctive Lafayette stamp.

Ireland, 1839–1900', i, 223–40.   **29** Cited in Slattery, 'The uses of photography in Ireland 1839–1900', i, 226.   **30** For examples of these prisoner photographs see Noel Kissane, *The Irish face* (Dublin, 1986), pp 58–9.   **31** Slattery, 'The uses of photography in Ireland 1839–1900', ii, Appendix B, pp 144–5.   **32** Cited in Chandler, *Photography in Ireland: the*

William Mervyn Lawrence (1840–1932) opened a photographic studio in 1865 in his mother's toy and fancy goods shop at 5–7 Upper Sackville Street, Dublin, just opposite the General Post Office. He was more businessman than photographer and presided over a very successful studio. At first stereographs were very popular and his studio catered for that demand. He was also a collector of photographs and bought the 2,900 glass negatives in the Eblana collection which were taken between 1870 and 1890 and the 300 glass plate negatives taken by Frederick Holland Mares in the 1860s. These and other acquisitions he made now form part of what is known as the 'Lawrence Collection'. He employed photographers, Robert French being the best known to travel around Ireland and to take pictures of virtually every town, village and scenic view in the country. His photographers were photojournalists of sorts, attempting to depict evictions and other aspects of the land war in the years 1879–82. The land war photographs are usually staged, after-the-event shots of people and damaged houses from which they have been evicted. Nevertheless, they are important and useful documents for historians researching this period. From the 1890s onwards he produced vast numbers of picture postcards depicting various scenes of landscapes and streetscapes around Ireland. All the portrait negatives in the Sackville Street studio were destroyed during Easter week 1916. Fortunately the glass negatives of outdoor views which were stored in Rathmines survived the rising.[33] The Lawrence Collection of approximately 40,000 glass negatives and 15,000 photographic prints is, because of its size, scope and quality of photographs, the most important nineteenth-century Irish photographic collection. It is housed in the National Photographic Archive in Temple Bar, Dublin.[34]

DOCUMENTARY PHOTOGRAPHY

Documentary photography was gaining in popularity in Ireland and elsewhere from the 1880s onwards. The smaller portable cameras with faster exposure times facilitated this kind of photography. Some photographers used their cameras to highlight the poverty and inequalities they saw in society. Leland Lewis Duncan (1862–1923), an Englishman who worked at the War Office in London, visited his cousins, the Slackes of Annadale, Co. Leitrim, in the summers between 1889 and 1894 and took approximately 200 photographs while there. He tried to document, with his camera and pen, what life was like in the rural north-west of Ireland at this time. In a systematic and methodical way he took pictures of each type of house from the poorest mud cabin to the big house as well as the people who lived in them. He photographed dolmens and abbey ruins, farm tools and meitheals, tenants

nineteenth century, p. 88.   **33** Rouse, *Into the light*, pp 54–6. For information on William Lawrence see Kieran Hickey, *The light of other days* (London, 1973); Chandler, *Photography in Ireland: the nineteenth century*, pp 58–61.   **34** To check the list of Lawrence photographs see the National Photographic Archive on line catalogue at http://www.nli.ie/onlinedatabases

2.4 Photograph from the Lawrence collection of the Cooperage area of Killarney, Co. Kerry, *c.*1890 (courtesy of National Photographic Archive)

and servants at the big house. He captioned his photographs, kept a diary and gathered folklore from the people he met. Owing to his meticulous documentary approach and the fact that he was taking photographs in a part of the country largely neglected by other photographers,[35] his pictures are of particular importance.[36]

William Fee McKinney (1832–1917), a substantial farmer and photographer, who lived in Carnmoney, Co. Antrim, took photographs in south Antrim during the period 1885 to 1910. His pictures are similar in many respects to Duncan's Leitrim pictures. McKinney, unlike Duncan, was a native of the area he photographed and he took pictures over a longer period and so built up a large photographic record of farming life in south Antrim at this time.[37] He took photographs not just of the big houses, but also of the one-roomed and two-roomed cottages and of the people who lived in them. He photographed the farm machinery, farm implements and farm sheds in an attempt to document a whole way of life. He also kept diaries, gathered ballads and, like Duncan, collected folklore. His house, called 'Sentry Hill', is now a heritage centre and is open to the

35 The Lawrence collection appears to have only one photograph taken in County Leitrim. **36** For information on Leland L. Duncan, see Liam Kelly, *The face of time: photographs of County Leitrim, 1889–94* (Dublin, 1995); Liam Kelly, *Kiltubrid, County Leitrim: snapshots of a rural parish in the 1890s* (Dublin, 2005).   **37** Approximately 600 of his glass negatives have

2.5 Photograph by Rose Shaw of Mary and Ellen McCaughey, Corleaghan, Co. Tyrone, *c.*1910 (RS 360) (courtesy of Ulster Folk and Transport Museum)

public.[38] The achievement of both Duncan and McKinney was that they broke the mould and photographed all aspects of life in two very different rural communities in south Leitrim and south Antrim towards the end of the Victorian era.

Rose Shaw took some wonderful photographs of women and other farm workers in the Clogher valley of Co. Tyrone in the early 1900s. Her photographs are more artistic than either Duncan's or McKinney's. Very few of her photographs have survived, though the quality of those that have are proof of the quality of her camera work. Thirty of her photographs are held in the Ulster Folk and Transport Museum in Hollywood, Co. Down.

William Cavanagh (1862–1952), a harness maker from New Ross, Co. Wexford, was taking photographs in New Ross and the south-east of Ireland at the same time that William McKinney was doing so in the north-east of the country. Cavanagh was an excellent photographer and had a particular interest in photographing early bicycles and motor cars. Anyone interested in the history of New Ross in the period 1890–1910 will find this collection an invaluable resource.[39]

survived.   **38** For more information on William F. McKinney and his photographs see Brian M. Walker, *Sentry Hill, an Ulster farm & family* (Belfast, 1981).   **39** I am indebted to Jimmy Fitzgibbon for his help and information on William Cavanagh. See Jimmy Fitzgibbon, *A time and place – New Ross, 1890–1910, a photographic record of the time* (New

The Kilkenny Archaeological Society, which was founded in 1849 and later became the Royal Society of Antiquaries of Ireland, took an early interest in photography – perhaps because Dr William Hemphill was a member of the society. A debate was conducted within the society as to the relative merits of drawings and photographs in illustrating buildings and other objects of interest to antiquarians. In 1891 the society took the decision to begin a photographic collection.[40] The photographer and antiquarian Thomas J. Westropp was honorary curator of the expanding photographic collection from 1893 until 1921. Photographers such as John L. Robinson, Samuel K. Kirker, Lord Walter Fitzgerald and Ephraim MacDowell Cosgrave contributed many images to the society's collection, which has continued to grow to the present day and now comprises more than 20,000 prints, glass plates and negative images taken all over Ireland.[41]

WELCH, HOGG AND GREEN

Three of the best photographers in Ireland in the late nineteenth and early twentieth century were Ulstermen. Robert J. Welch (1859–1936) was the most important and prolific photographer in the north of Ireland at this time. His work, much like that of the Lawrence studio in Dublin, helped the spread of photography throughout the country.[42] Born in Strabane, Co. Tyrone and resident for a time in Enniskillen where his father had a photographic studio, in 1875 Welch moved to Belfast and worked for the photographer E.T. Church before setting up his own studio in Lonsdale Street in 1883. He had a keen eye and his photographs attest to his interests in archaeology, architecture, history, botany and zoology. Welch was the official photographer to Harland and Wolff shipping company[43] and to the Belfast Rope-works Company and his pictures of these companies and of the linen industry are very important images of the industrialized north-east, particularly for the period from 1885 until the First World War. He travelled extensively throughout Ireland taking photographs wherever he went. Most of his pictures are of Ulster and western Connacht though he did take photographs as far south as Kerry. A large number of his images are housed in the Ulster Museum, Botanic Gardens, Belfast, but approximately 400 of his photographs are in the Sir Benjamin Stone Collection in Birmingham Central Library. He was elected to the Royal Irish Academy in 1903 and he was awarded an honorary degree by Queen's University, Belfast in 1923 in recognition of his contribution to photography.

Ross, 2007). **40** *Journal of the Royal Society of Antiquaries of Ireland*, 23 (1890–1), p. 712. **41** I am indebted to Chris Corlett, honorary librarian of the Royal Society of Antiquaries of Ireland, for this information on the photographic collections at RSAI. He is currently gathering and cataloguing their vast collection. **42** E.E. Evans & B.S. Turner, *Ireland's eye, the photographs of Robert John Welch* (Belfast, 1996); See also articles by Vivienne Pollock, Gail Baylis, Ciarán Walsh and Lorna Moloney in Ciara Breathnach (ed.), *Framing the west, images of rural Ireland, 1891–1920* (Dublin, 2007). **43** There is a collection of approximately 8,000 Harland & Wolff photographs in the Ulster Folk & Transport Museum in Hollywood,

2.6 Photograph by William A. Green of turf-walled cabin in Co. Antrim, *c.*1910 (WAG 269)
(courtesy of Ulster Folk and Transport Museum)

Alexander Hogg (1870–1939), a native of Co. Down, developed his skills with
lantern slides and camera before setting up a photographic studio in Trinity Street
in Belfast in 1901. His earliest surviving picture was taken in 1888, though most of
the photographs in his collection were taken during the first three decades of the
twentieth century. He took pictures of Belfast's industrial life and its public
buildings and slum dwellings; he also photographed farming life in Co. Antrim and
of the scenic views in the north-east of the country. His collection of approximately
5,000 glass plate negatives, 1,500 lantern slides and his account books are held in
the Ulster Museum.[44]

William Alfred Green (1870–1958) was born into a tea merchant family in
Newry, Co. Down. He worked as an apprentice photographer with Robert J. Welch
before setting up his own studio in Belfast in 1910. He moved his studio to Antrim
town in 1924. A meticulous photographer with a keen interest in history and
folklore, he is best known for his photographs showing the minutiae of farming life
in the Toome area of Co. Antrim. Many of his photographs, depicting streetscapes,
public buildings and scenic views, were sold as picture postcards. He had a keen eye
and his pictures are evidence of his interest in local history and folk culture. His

County Down. Michael McCaughan, *Steel ships and iron men: shipbuilding in Belfast, 1894–1912*
(Belfast, 1989).   **44** For information on Alexander Hogg see W.A. Maguire, *Caught in time:
the photographs of Alexander Hogg of Belfast, 1870–1939* (Belfast, 1986).

photographs cover the period 1895 to 1935. They can be identified by his trademark initials WAG and they were taken mostly, though not exclusively, in Ulster. A total of 4,114 of his plate glass negatives are in the Ulster Folk & Transport Museum at Hollywood in Co. Down.[45]

POSTCARDS

The growth in photography in Ireland accelerated greatly in the early 1900s because of the popularity of picture postcards. Various types of postcards were printed from 1860 onwards both in Europe and in the United States. The early postcards usually had lithographs on one side with the other side taken up completely with the receiver's name and address. The message sent by postcard was written over the lithographic image. In the 1890s photographs replaced the lithographs to create pictorial cards, later called picture postcards. In 1902 the British Postmaster-General gave permission for postcards to have a divided back with one half for the written message and the other for the address.[46] With this development the picture postcard became very popular and the period from 1902 to 1914 is generally recognized as the heyday of the postcard/photograph, though they continued to be popular until the middle of the twentieth century.

The main photographic firms supplying postcards in Ireland were the Lawrence studio, Eason & Son Ltd, Valentine & Son, and Hely's Ltd who were based in Dame Street, in Dublin.[47] Local photographic studios such as J.A. Coleman's studio in Bailieborough, Co. Cavan, which was established in 1904, sold 'postcards of Bailieboro and district, including all the places of interest … together with many other places of note in Co. Cavan'.[48] The early Irish postcards usually depicted streetscapes, scenic landscapes, public buildings and historic sites and consequently they are important documents for local historians researching the early decades of the twentieth century.[49] Gradually as the century progressed postcards became glossy and colourful and projected a more romanticized view of Ireland, with the result that these postcards are less useful to the historian than the earlier black-and-white postcard photographs of the towns and villages of Ireland.

45 T.K. Anderson, 'William Alfred Green FRSAI: the man and his photographs' in *Ulster Local Studies*, 14, no. 2 (Winter 1991), pp 18–29; Jane E.M. Crosbie, *A tour of North Down, 1895–1925: historic photographs from the W.A. Green collection at the Ulster Folk & Transport Museum* (Belfast, 1989); Doreen Corcoran, *A tour of East Antrim: historic photographs from the W.A. Green collection in the Ulster Folk & Transport Museum* (Belfast, 1990). **46** Eric Jevans & Jeffrey Richards, *A social history of Britain in postcards 1870–1930* (London, 1980), p. 4; S. Kearns, *1894–1994: The centenary of the picture postcard in Ireland*, Guinness Hop Store Exhibition, Dublin (Dublin, 1994); Ian Baird, 'Collecting old postcards' in the *Irish Independent*, 24 Mar. 2001. **47** Niall Murphy, *A Bloomsday postcard* (Dublin, 2004), pp 28–9. **48** Maguire, *A century in focus*, p. 83. **49** They are particularly useful for those researching the built environment. For examples of the type of postcard photographs available see P.J. Dunne, *County Cavan in old picture postcards, with historical commentary* (Cavan, 2000). The text

2.7 Thomas J. Wynne advertising his photographic studio in Castlebar, Co. Mayo (WYN1)[50] (courtesy of National Photographic Archive)

is by Dr Ciaran Parker. See also T. Cadogan, *Cobh in old picture postcards* (Zaltbommel, 1995). The Cardall photographic collection in the National Photographic Archive consists of *c.*5,000 postcard photographs of 218 towns and villages in Ireland taken in the 1940s and 1950s. **50** Photographers and shopkeepers regularly used photographs to advertise their business. See the photograph of John Couch's photographic agency shop at 6 Eustace Street, Dublin, taken *c.*1865 in Chandler, *Photography in Ireland*, p. 48.

REGIONAL PHOTOGRAPHIC STUDIOS

By the end of the nineteenth century virtually every town in Ireland had a resident photographer who very often had another line of business such as a chemist, newsagent or hardware shop. They took studio pictures of individuals, family groups and primary school groups as well as photographs of streetscapes, landscapes and the built environment – some of which were intended to be sold commercially in the locality as postcards.[51] Perhaps the best known and most important of these regional photographers was Thomas J. Wynne (1838–93). A newsagent in Castlebar, Co. Mayo, he began taking photographs in the town in 1867. Later generations of the Wynne family continued with the photography business and in 1993 presented the National Library with a collection consisting of c.8,000 glass negative images of various aspects of life in Castlebar and in other parts of Co. Mayo between the years 1867 and 1960. This important collection is now held in the National Photographic Archive in Temple Bar. The remaining Wynne images are housed in the Mayo County Library in Castlebar.

Robert Day (1836–1914) was president of Cork Historical and Archaeological Society and a gifted photographer. He took many pictures of his native city of Cork from c.1860 to his death in 1914. Most of his best pictures were taken in the period 1890 to 1910. Robert's son William (1874–1965) inherited his father's interest in photography and took many images of Cork in the early decades of the twentieth century. William's son, Alec (1902–80), continued the family's photographic tradition for a third generation and helped form the Cork Camera Club in 1923.[52] These three photographers from the Day family have built up an important photographic collection of Cork city and its people. The earlier photographs in this collection depict mostly streetscapes while the later ones show a city bustling with people and commerce.[53] This collection is held in the Local Studies section of Cork City Library.

The family firm of A.H. Poole had a photographic studio in Waterford city from 1884 to 1954 and in that period amassed a collection of c.65,000 glass negatives.[54] This large and important collection is now in the National Photographic Archive in Dublin. Many of the images are portraits of individuals and groups from Waterford and the south-east. However, this vast collection also includes several important images of the built environment, the social, cultural and commercial life of Waterford city, New Ross, Tramore and parts of south Co. Kilkenny which are adjacent to Waterford. The National Photographic Archives has 120 note books which help to identify and date the photographs in this collection.

51 For example Mrs M.A. Canning, who had a confectionary shop, in Dromahair, County Leitrim, published and sold postcards depicting O'Rourke's Castle in Dromahair. I am indebted to P.J. Dunne for giving me one of these postcards.   **52** The Cork Camera Club website which shows 56 images from the Day collection is http://www.corkpastandpresent.ie/corkimages/camera_club.shtml (19 Nov. 2006).   **53** Colin Rynne & Billy Wigham, *Forgotten Cork: photographs from the Day collection* (Cork, 2004).   **54** Rouse, *Into the light*, p. 74. Des

2.8 Photograph by A.H. Poole taken in Burnamahon, Co. Waterford, *c.*1910 (PWP 1578) (courtesy of National Photographic Archive)

THE CONGESTED DISTRICTS BOARD

The Congested Districts Board[55] was set up in August 1891 under Arthur Balfour's 'Purchase of Land Act'. According to the terms of this act, parts of the west of Ireland stretching from Donegal to Kerry were designated 'congested' or impoverished districts. Inspectors were sent into these areas to draw up detailed reports on the conditions of the people living there. Their 'baseline reports' give a good insight into the living conditions of people who lived in rural areas along the western seaboard. Their reports were, in some instances, supplemented by photographs, most of which were taken in the period 1895–1914. These are important documentary photographs taken mostly in isolated rural areas and depicting the people, houses, dress, farm tools and fishing gear. The Belfast-based photographer, Robert J. Welch, took approximately 105 of the 120 images in the Congested Districts Board collection.[56] Other photographs in this collection were

Griffin, *A parcel from the past: Waterford as seldom seen before* (Waterford, 1994).   **55** William L. Micks, *An account of the constitution, administration and dissolution of the Congested Districts Board from 1889 to 1923* (Dublin, 1925); James Morrissey (ed.), *On the verge of want* (Dublin, 2001); Ciara Breathnach, *The Congested Districts Board of Ireland, 1891–1923* (Dublin, 2005). See articles by Justin Carville and Jonathan Bell in Breathnach (ed.), *Framing the west.* **56** Rouse, *Into the light*, pp 18–19.

taken by J.D. Cassidy, a photographer from Ardara, Co. Donegal. This is a small collection but because of the quality and the documentary nature of the images, it is a very important one. The Congested Districts Board photographic collection is available for consultation in the National Photographic Archive in Temple Bar.

Major Robert Rutledge-Fair was one of the inspectors employed by the Congested Districts Board in Co. Galway. At the request of James H. Tuke, an English Quaker and philanthropist who worked with the poor in the west of Ireland, Rutledge-Fair took excellent documentary photographs of life in Connemara in 1892. This collection, which has recently been acquired by the National Photographic Archive, is similar in many respects and as important as the Congested Districts Board photographic collection.

AUTOCROME PHOTOGRAPHS

Two young Frenchwomen, Marguerite Mespoulet and Madeleine Mignon-Alba, visited Ireland in 1913 and took excellent documentary photographs in Galway city and county, Clonmacnoise, Athlone, Glendalough, Newgrange and Co. Louth. Their work in Ireland was part of a larger project sponsored Albert Kahn, a French banker and philanthropist, who sent teams of photographers to fifty countries throughout the world in the hope that by building up a large collection of photographs of different races and cultures he would promote reconciliation and harmony. Between the years 1909 and 1931 his photographers amassed a collection of 72,000 photographs. Mespoulet and Mignon-Alba used the recently developed autochrome process which meant that colour photographs could be directly reproduced for the first time. Their photographs, the earliest and most important colour photographs taken in Ireland, are part of the 'Archives of the planet' collection and are held in the Albert Kahn museum, at 14 Rue du Port, Boulogne-Billancourt in Paris.[57] The journal which these two French photographers kept during their time in Ireland gives useful background information about their pictures. It too is held in the Kahn museum in Paris.

PRESS PHOTOGRAPHY

At the beginning of the twentieth century the manufacture of printing plates on metal by half-tone engraving, and later the transmission of photographs by wire, led to a rapid increase in the use of photography by newspapers.[58] The growth in the use of photographs in newspapers to supplement and illustrate the printed word

57 Approximately 50 of their photographs were on display in an exhibition called 'In search of Ireland in 1913' in Galway City Museum from June to September 2007. See article 'Peaceful pictures on the eve of war' by Lorna Siggins in the *Irish Times*, 19 June 2007. **58** Pierre Albert & Gilles Feyel, 'Photography and the media' in Frizot, *The new history of*

2.9 An *Irish Independent* photograph of Michael Collins's coffin being loaded onto a gun carriage on 28 August 1922[59] (courtesy of National Photographic Archive)

was hindered in Ireland as elsewhere by the outbreak of war in 1914. As a result it was not until after the First World War that newspapers began to include photographs as a matter of course. However, some newspapers have photographic archive material dating back to the early years of the twentieth century.

William Martin Murphy leased premises in Middle Abbey Street in Dublin in 1904 for the production of a new daily newspaper and the first issue of the *Irish Independent* rolled off the presses on 2 January 1905. One hundred years later, in October 2005, the National Photographic Archive hosted an exhibition entitled 'A century of news photography' to mark the centenary of the *Irish Independent*. The previous year the paper had donated all of its photographic archive to the National Library of Ireland. This very large collection of approximately 300,000 items has yet to be sorted and catalogued. The photographs for the early years of the newspapers are scarce and there are some obvious gaps, even in more recent years. There are, however, important pictures in the collection of the 1916 Rising, the War of Independence and the Civil War – and of virtually every newsworthy event in the country since then. The *Irish Times*, too, has a large photographic archive and photographs taken since September 2001 may be accessed and ordered on-line.[60]

Press photographers and photo-journalists have between them created a very large volume of excellent photographs which should be a rich source of information for

photography, p. 359.   **59** http://www.ireland.com/photosales (30 May 2007).   **60** For other pictures of Michael Collins see Chrissy Osborne, *Michael Collins: a life in pictures* (Cork, 2007).

historians. A good example are the photographs of Colman Doyle who became a staff photographer with the *Irish Press* in 1951. His photographs were taken throughout Ireland in the second half of the twentieth century. They are informative and visually striking and they depict the social, political and sporting life of the country. His photographs of 'The Troubles' in northern Ireland are among the best available.[61] Local historians may find the images created by local or regional press photographers especially helpful. For example Stan Shields, who was photographer with *The Connacht Tribune* from 1960 to 2000, built up a large collection of excellent photographs which may be more useful to local historians in the west of Ireland than many of the images published in the national newspapers.[62]

Researchers need to check with local newspapers to see if they hold a photographic archive of the images they published in their paper. Very often they employed free-lance photographers and in many instances it is they who hold the collections. Some of these collections have been given to local museums or libraries. Most, however, are still held privately.

FR FRANK BROWNE

Frank Browne, Ireland's most important photographer, was born in the year 1880 into a well-off family in Cork city. In 1897 he entered the seminary as a Jesuit novice. He studied classics at the Royal University of Ireland at St Stephen's Green later studying theology in Italy before he was ordained priest in 1915. He became a chaplain with the First Battalion of the Irish Guards and served on the front line in France and Flanders until the war ended in 1918, winning the Military Cross and other awards for bravery.[63] He returned to Dublin where he was based for the rest of his life. A good preacher, he travelled around Ireland giving retreats and parish missions. He is best known now for his photographs. He travelled on the *Titanic* on the first two stages of its fateful journey from Southampton to Cherbourg and then on to Queenstown. The photographs he took while on the *Titanic* became hugely significant after the *Titanic* sank and they catapulted a budding photographer into the limelight.[64]

When Frank Browne died in 1960 he left behind a legacy of approximately 42,000 negatives, neatly captioned and precariously stored – remarkable shots taken, mostly in Ireland, over the previous half century.[65] He took photographs in every county in Ireland, bringing his camera with him on his preaching missions. A

---

61 Colman Doyle, *All changed: fifty years of photographing Ireland* (Dublin, 2004). The text is by John Quinn. **62** Stan Shields, *Stan's Galway* (Dublin, 2006). **63** His photograph 'With the Irish Guards at the Somme', showing the dead and injured, captures some of the horror and chaos of war. E.E. O'Donnell, *Father Browne, a life in pictures* (Dublin, 1994), p. 49. **64** For details of Fr Browne's life see O'Donnell, *Father Browne: a life in pictures*. **65** Some of the photographs in the Browne Collection were taken in England, Scotland, Wales and Australia. Approximately 35,000 of the photographs were taken in Ireland.

2.10 Photograph by Fr Frank Browne taken at Cooraclare creamery, Co. Clare in 1944 (courtesy of Irish Picture Library)

prolific and gifted photographer, his pictures are informative, quirky and artistic. He has been compared to the famous French photographer Henri Cartier-Bresson who perfected the art of snap shooting his pictures and choosing exactly the right moment to do so. Browne and Cartier-Bresson both believed that even the smallest detail, the ordinary things that others see yet never notice, can make the greatest picture.[66] David H. Davison's testifies to the unique value of the Browne collection:

> There is no other collection of twentieth-century Irish photography of such stature, none so large, so wide in range of subject or rival in terms of artistic achievement. Fr Browne's work is not just of significance for Ireland: I believe that as it becomes more widely known he will be acknowledged as one of the great photographers of the first half of this century.[67]

Another Jesuit priest, Fr E.E. O'Donnell, took an active interest in the Browne collection, which he first came across in 1985. He secured sponsorship from Allied Irish Bank and expert help, from David and Edwin Davison, in rescuing the

66 Henri Cartier-Bresson, *The decisive moment: photographs by Henri Cartier-Bresson* (New York, 1952). This book may be found on line at http://e-photobooks.com/cartier-bresson/ decisive-moment.html   **67** O'Donnell, *Father Browne: a life in pictures*, p. 124. David H. Davison is the retired head of the Department of Photography at the Dublin Institute of Technology and is a member of the Irish Professional Conservators and Restorers Association.

collection. He has published 22 volumes of Fr Browne's photographs and helped to preserve and publicize his work.[68] This very large collection, which covers the whole country, is an important resource for local historians researching the first half of the twentieth century. It is held by the Irish Picture Library at 69B Heather Road, Sandyford, Dublin 18.[69]

Hugh Doran (1926–2004) was another talented amateur photographer. He worked for Guinness's brewery and practised photography in his spare time. He joined the Photographic Society of Ireland in 1949 and from the mid-1950s his pictures were exhibited in Ireland and in many European cities. He photographed Dublin city and had a particular interest in portraits and in architecture. In 1959, at the request of Desmond Guinness, he photographed Irish town and country houses for an Irish Georgian Society exhibition. His black-and-white photographs, in which he makes wonderful use of natural light, are testament to his great talent. His wife Kitty donated his collection to the Irish Architectural Archives at 45 Merrion Square, Dublin, in 2005.[70] An exhibition of his photographs was held by the IAA in August 2007 and a book, *Hugh Doran, photographer*, was published to coincide with that exhibition.

TRAINS AND AEROPLANES

The camera and the steam engine train came of age together in the nineteenth century. Photographers, especially those who used the early bulky cameras, often depended on the train to get around. Historians trying to understand why photographers took shots in one place and not in another should check contemporary maps for roads and railroads. The fact that Leland L. Duncan took photographs in the rather remote Arigna mining valley on the Leitrim/ Roscommon border in 1889 but did not take any in the county town of Carrick-on-Shannon can be explained by the fact that he depended on the Cavan, Leitrim & Roscommon Light Railway for transport.[71] Photographers liked trains, not just as a means of transport, but also as objects to be photographed. Consequently a large volume of photographs of trains and railways stations has been amassed here in Ireland. James P. O'Dea (1910–66) was a founding member of the Irish Railways Record Society and his photographs. taken between 1937 and 1966, comprise one of the largest and best known Irish collection of rail-related photographs. It may be consulted in the National Photographic Archives in Dublin. There are many other smaller collections. Most local libraries have photographs of the railways systems that existed in their areas.

Just as trains helped the growth of photography in the nineteenth century, aeroplanes did so in the twentieth century. The Parisian photographer Felix Nadar

68 For a full listing of E.E. O'Donnell's books containing Frank Browne's photographs see the bibliography below. **69** See contact details in next section listing photographic collections. **70** For contact details see below for list of photographic collections. **71** Kelly, *The face of time*,

took aerial photographs from a hot air balloon as early as 1858 and by 1903 Julius Neubronne had patented a breast-mounted, timer-controlled camera for homing pigeons which literally gave a bird's-eye view of what lay below. It was, however, during the First World War that aerial photography, which relied on aeroplanes to be airborne, developed rapidly to meet the military needs of the time. During the 1920s and 1930s the Royal Air Force took aerial photographs of the north of Ireland. Many of the aerial photographs from this period are located in the Department of the Environment for Northern Ireland, though some are to be found in the Ulster Folk and Transport Museum.[72] There are approximately 1,500 aerial photographs of archaeological sites and historic buildings in Northern Ireland, taken between 1944 and 1959, in the Public Records Office of Northern Ireland. The aerial photographs taken during the two world wars were for military purposes and consequently are mostly of cities, ports, airports and other strategic places. Many of the photographs taken in northern Ireland after the Second World War were taken by retired RAF pilots for various government departments to depict towns, landscape, forestry and lakes.

On 29 December 1940, five months before they dropped bombs on the city, the German Luftwaffe took aerial pictures of the military barracks and other public buildings in Dublin.[73] In the period 1954–57 Captain Alexander Campbell Morgan (1920–58), who had been a reconnaissance pilot with the Royal Artillery in the Second World War, established a company called 'Aerophotos' and set about photographing much of Ireland from the air. His collection of 2,831 negatives, held in the National Photographic Archives, are detailed black-and-white aerial shots of every county in Ireland which were taken from medium- and low-altitude flights.[74] Captain Morgan's photographic work ended abruptly when he was killed in a plane crash near Shannon airport in January 1958.[75] Keith Saint Joseph took aerial photographs in Britain and Ireland in the 1950s and 1960s. His photographs are to be found in Cambridge University Library.[76] Rex Roberts also took some excellent oblique photographs of Ireland. Between 1973 and 1977 the Geological Survey of Ireland photographed all of the Republic of Ireland from the air. Even though their black-and-white photographs were taken from a height of 15,000 feet and were intended for use by geologists and geographers, they can be of use to historians too.

Since the mid-1960s the Ordnance Survey of Ireland (OS*i*) has undergone many technological changes and has now a sophisticated system in place for supplying maps and other documents, including aerial photographs, relating to all areas within the Republic of Ireland. The OS*i* has amassed a large collection of aerial

p. 51.   **72** Maguire, *A century in focus*, p. 141.   **73** Copies of 16 of these photographs are in the National Photographic Archives.   **74** Noel Kissane (ed.), *Ex camera 1860–1960: photographs from the collections of the National Library of Ireland* (Dublin, 1994), pp 78–9, 96; K. Dwyer, *Ireland: our island home* (Cork, 1997); B. Kiely, *The aerofilms book of Ireland – from the air* (London, 1985); D. Pochin-Mould, *Ireland from the air* (Belfast, 1972).   **75** Rouse, *Into the light*, p. 64.   **76** The contact details for the aerial photographic collections in Cambridge University Library are: email: library@uflm.cam.ac.uk or tel.: 01223 764377.

2.11 Aerial view of Aran islands, *c.*1980 (courtesy of National Photographic Archive)

photographs, the earliest of which are black and white while many of the more recent pictures are in colour. The collection includes high-flown, small-scale photographs of every county taken at three different times – in the 1970s, 1995 and 2000. These vertical survey photographs are most useful for identifying earthworks and larger sites of historical interest. Low-flown or oblique flights are best for smaller sites such as ring-barrows. The Ordnance Survey of Ireland also has many medium- and low-flown aerial photographs, taken in the period 1970–2000, which are important and useful documents for historians and archaeologists.

The Ordnance Survey of Northern Ireland (OS*ni*) has been taking aerial photographs since 1959 and has built up a collection of approximately 500,000 photographs. Cities and towns and forested areas feature prominently in this collection. Virtually all of the six counties are included. Most of the photographs are medium- and low-flown oblique views. The photographs from the 1960s and 70s are mostly black and white. Those taken in more recent years are in colour. This collection is held by OSNI in Colby House in Belfast.[77]

---

77 For contact details see the list of photographic collections below.

Rapid growth in the number of aeroplanes and the increasing sophistication of cameras has meant that aerial photography has developed greatly since the 1960s. Since the early 1990s, with the building of new motorways, power lines and pipelines and the consequent threat to historical and archaeological sites, the photographing of these sites from the air has continued unabated. In the years 2003 to 2005 the National Inventory of Archaeological Heritage gathered *c*.6,000 aerial photographs of big houses and historic gardens in Ireland. This project has shown how aerial photographs and maps can, with the same scale and orientation, be usefully studied alongside one another.[78]

Aerial photography has been very important for historians and has helped greatly in identifying significant archaeological sites throughout the country. Several unrecorded field monuments in west Wicklow were discovered by using the Google Earth website.[79] This website uses satellite images, aerial photography and the Geographical Information System to give a bird's-eye view of the landscape. It is estimated that 65% of the ring-barrows in Co. Limerick were identified through aerial photography.[80] It can also be a very useful source for historians since, unlike ground photography, it gives a wide perspective and helps put the object or area being studied into context. One of the weaknesses of ground photography is that a single photograph can be accurately described as a rather small fragment of a much larger picture. Aerial photography gives a broader perspective and helps put archaeological sites or historical monuments into the context of their surrounding landscape. Aerial photography has its weaknesses too. It needs to be accompanied by thorough field-work. Where there is extensive undergrowth or when the weather is bad, it is largely ineffective. Despite these drawbacks, historians will in the future make more use of the vast collections of aerial photographs which have been built up mostly, though not exclusively, in the last half century.

Many photographers living abroad have contributed both in quality and quantity to the photographic collections relating to Ireland. Among them are two New York-based photographers, Alen MacWeeney and Jill Freedman. Alen MacWeeney was born in Dublin in 1939 and began working as a press photographer with the *Irish Times* in 1955. In 1961 he moved to New York where he established himself as one of the most talented photographers of his time.[81] He continued to visit Ireland regularly and to take good photographs of various aspects of Irish life. His photographs include images of inner city life in Dublin, of the travelling community,[82] country life and landscapes. Jill Freedman, a writer and freelance photographer, was fascinated with Ireland and took exceptional photographs on her visits to Ireland since the 1970s. She was particularly interested

78 National Inventory of Archaeological Heritage, http://www.buildingsofireland.ie (9 Feb. 2007).   **79** The website address is http://earth.google.com See C.J. Darby, 'Googling the landscape: discovering a prehistoric landscape in west Wicklow' in *Archaeology Ireland* (Winter 2007), pp 20–3.   **80** http://www.heritagecouncil.ie (8 Dec. 2006).   **81** For an assessment of Alen MacWeeney's work see Jussim, *The eternal moment*, pp 135–40.   **82** Alen MacWeeney, *Irish travellers: tinkers no more* (Henniker, NH, 2007); Alen MacWeeney & Richard Conniff, *Irish walls* (New York, 1986); Alen MacWeeney & Sue Allison, *Bloomsbury*

in life off the beaten track in the west of Ireland. Her images of musicians, drinkers, dancers and farming people in the west captured a way of life that was rapidly dying out.[83] Christy McNamara, a musician and photographer from Co. Clare, has also taken many excellent photographs of Irish musicians.[84]

The north-east of Ireland, especially the counties of Antrim and Down, has been documented by several talented photographers. William McKinney, Robert Welch, Alexander Hogg and William Green were creating exceptional photographs of people and place in these counties in the last decades of the nineteenth century and the early decades of the twentieth century. In the years before, during and after the Second World War the Kilkeel area of Co. Down produced two more talented photographers in Pat Hudson and Ben Corr. Hudson took photographs of farmers and fishermen in south Down in the years 1930 to 1945 while Ben Corr, who worked for the Ministry of Agriculture, was excellently placed to take photographs, mostly of the farming community, in the Mourne district between the years 1955 and 1975.[85]

Since 1839 there have been cameras and photographers producing photographic images in Ireland. This short guide can only refer to some of them. In the early decades of photography much of the work was experimental and photography was only for the few who had the knowledge and the money to do so. Then as the camera became easier to use and cheaper to buy, the volume of photographs produced increased accordingly. There is now, almost 170 years after the camera was invented, an incredibly large volume of photographic images relating to Ireland. An increasing number of these images are held in the National Photographic Archives in Dublin or in other public archives, libraries or museums throughout Ireland. There are, however, large and significant collections of photographs in private hands, some of which are in a precarious state. Local historians, together with the local studies libraries, have an important role to play in unearthing these photographs, securing, preserving, identifying, dating and cataloguing them.

reflection (New York, 1990).   **83** Jill Freedman, *A time that was: Irish moments* (London, 1987); idem, *Ireland ever* (New York, 2005).   **84** Christy McNamara & Peter Wood, *The living note: the heartbeat of Irish music* (Dublin, 1996); Siobhán Long, 'The sounds and the visions' in *Irish Times*, 5 Oct. 2007.   **85** Ben Corr, *From the mountains to the sea: photographs of the people of Mourne, 1955–75* (Belfast, 1989).

CHAPTER 3

Some photographic collections relating to Ireland

This chapter lists some of the photographic collections in public repositories which may be of interest to local historians in Ireland. It does not claim to be a complete list. It will, however, give researchers some idea of the type of photographic collections that are available and where they may be found. A considerable number are in the National Photographic Archives in Dublin. Sarah Rouse's excellent guide *Into the light: an illustrated guide to the photographic collections in the National Library of Ireland* (Dublin, 1998) should be consulted for more information on the collections in the National Photographic Archives, though others acquired in the last nine years are not listed in it. Many collections and photographs of historical interest are still in private hands here in Ireland or abroad. Historians, therefore, will need to cast a wide net when trawling for photographic documentation.

The format for each entry is as follows: the name of collection, the period in which the photographs were taken, approximate number of images in the collection, a brief description of photographs and finally the name, address, telephone number (from the Republic of Ireland) and email address of the library, archive or museum where the collection is held.

Adair Collection

1900–28 *c*.75 photographs

These images are part of the estate papers of the Adair family from Donegore, Co. Antrim.

Public Records Office of Northern Ireland, 66 Balmoral Avenue, Belfast BT9 6NY. Tel.: 028 90255905. Email: proni@dcalni.gov.uk

Allen Library Collection

1900–2000

Miscellaneous photographs relating to prominent Irish literary and political figures.

Allen Library, Edmund Rice House, North Richmond Street, Dublin 1. Tel.: 01 8551077. Email: allenlib@connect.ie

Allison Family Collection

1900–39

Good collection of photographs of life in Ulster – though mainly of Armagh city and county.

Public Records Office of Northern Ireland, 66 Balmoral Avenue, Belfast BT9 6NY. Tel.: 028 90255905. Email: proni@dcalni.gov.uk

Anderson, Samuel Lee

1865–71   204 photographic prints

Mug shots of Fenians, Ribbonmen and other prisoners.

National Photographic Archive, Meeting House Square, Temple Bar, Dublin 2.

Tel.: 01 6030371. Email: photoarchive@nli.ie

Annesley Collection

1855–95   35 albums of photographs

Important early photographs taken by Hugh, fifth earl of Annesley, in Co. Down.[1]

Public Records Office of Northern Ireland, 66 Balmoral Avenue, Belfast BT9 6NY.

Tel.: 028 90255905. Email: proni@dcalni.gov.uk

Athlone Collection

1900–2000

Miscellaneous photographs of Athlone and surrounding areas.[2]

Aidan Heavey Public Library, Athlone Civic Centre, Church Street, Athlone, Co. Westmeath.

Tel.: 090 6442157. Email: athlib@westmeathcoco.ie

Bigger, F.J.

1890–1920

Photographs taken by the Belfast antiquarian who had an interest in coastal history and archaeology of Ulster and Connaught.

Ulster Museum, Botanic Gardens, Belfast, BT9 5AB.

Tel.: 028 90383000. For information and to contact museum see http://www.ulster museum.org.uk

Birr Castle Collection

1850–1880

Copy prints of photographs by Mary, countess of Rosse and others relating to Birr Castle.[3]

Irish Picture Library. 69B Heather Road, Sandyford Industrial Estate, Dublin 18.

Tel.: 01 2950799. Email: ipl@fatherbrowne.com

Blake-Forster Collection

1860–80   *c.*100 photographic prints

Built environment and portraits taken in Co. Galway.

National Photographic Archive, Meeting House Square, Temple Bar, Dublin 2.

Tel.: 01 6030371. Email: photoarchive@nli.ie

---

1 The photographic albums are part of the Annesley estate papers in PRONI.   **2** Gearóid O'Brien, *Athlone in old photographs* (Dublin, 2002).   **3** For more information on the Birr photographs and on early photography visit Birr Castle, Birr, County Offaly. Tel.: 057 9120336. Email: mail@birrcastle.com

Bluett, Bill

1940–70

These photographs depict people, events and places in Co. Clare.[4]

Clare County Library, Mill Road, Ennis, Co. Clare.

Tel.: 065 6821616. Email: mailbox@clarelibrary.ie

Boyne Viaduct

1931–32   175 photographic prints

Images taken during repair work to Great Northern Railway viaduct over the river Boyne.

National Photographic Archive, Meeting House Square, Temple Bar, Dublin 2.

Tel.: 01 6030371. Email: photoarchive@nli.ie

Brophy, Annie

1922–78   60,000 negatives and prints

Portraits of individuals and families, streetscapes, built environment and other photographs relating mostly to Waterford City.[5]

Waterford City Archives, High Street, Waterford.

Tel.: 051 843123. Email: archives@waterfordcity.ie

Browne, Charles R.

1894   25 photographic prints and 22 photolithographs

Documentary pictures taken in Muingerena, Mullet, Iniskea and Portnacloy in west Mayo.

National Photographic Archive, Meeting House Square, Temple Bar, Dublin 2.

Tel.: 01 6030371. Email: photoarchive@nli.ie

Browne, Frank

1895–1955   *c.*41,500 monochrome photographs

Large collection of exceptional photographs taken all over Ireland by this Jesuit priest and photographer.[6]

Irish Picture Library, 69B Heather Road, Sandyford Industrial Estate, Dublin 18.

Tel.: 01 2950799. Email: helpdesk@fatherbrowne.com

Cardall Postcards

1940–60   *c.*5,000 photographic prints and negatives

Views of 218 towns and villages in Ireland.

National Photographic Archive, Meeting House Square, Temple Bar, Dublin 2.

Tel.: 01 6030371. Email: photoarchive@nli.ie

---

4 P. McNamara, 'The Lawrence photographs: Clare 1880–1910' in *Dal gCais*, 4 (1978), pp 5–9.   **5** Catherine Foley, 'Captured in place and time' in *Irish Times*, 19 May 2007. **6** For information on the photographer see O'Donnell, *Father Browne, a life in pictures*. For samples of the Fr Browne photographs see http://www.fatherbrowne.com. For a full listing of O'Donnell's books containing photographs from the Browne collection see the bibliography below.

Carrigan, William

1850–1900   63 photographs
Miscellaneous photographs of historic building in Co. Kilkenny – mostly relating to the life and work of Canon William Carrigan.
Library Headquarters, 6 Rose Inn Street, Kilkenny.
Tel.: 056 7794160. Email: info@kilkennylibrary.ie

Casement, Roger

1890–1916   *c.*175 photographic prints
Some of the images depict Roger Casement, his family and scenes from the Donegal Gaeltacht.
National Photographic Archive, Meeting House Square, Temple Bar, Dublin 2.
Tel.: 01 6030371. Email: photoarchive@nli.ie

Cashman, Joseph

1913–66
Important images of political figures and historic events in Ireland by this Dublin photographer.
RTÉ Stills Library. For information and to order see http://www.rte.ie/laweb/ll/ll_stills.html

Castletown, Lord

1860–1914   54 photographic prints and 35 negatives
Mostly studio portraits and miscellaneous big house scenes.
National Photographic Archive, Meeting House Square, Temple Bar, Dublin 2.
Tel.: 01 6030371. Email: photoarchive@nli.ie

Cavan Collection

1870–2000   *c.*4,000 photographic prints
Miscellaneous photographs of towns, villages and public buildings in Co. Cavan.
Johnston Central Library and Farnham Centre, Farnham Street, Cavan.
Tel.: 049 4378500. Email: b.connolly@cavancoco.ie

Cavanagh, William G.

1890–1910   *c.* 2,000 glass plate negatives (full plates and half plates)
Images of early cycling, motoring and other views of people and places in New Ross. Also holiday images from Tramore and Isle of Man.[7]
Jimmy Fitzgibbon, Marazion, Dowsley's Barn, New Ross, Co. Wexford.
Tel.: 051 421411

7 Jimmy Fitzgibbon, *A time and a place – New Ross 1890–1910, a photographic record of the time* (New Ross, 2007).

Ceannt, Áine
1925–38   10 photographic prints
Miscellaneous pictures which belonged to the wife of Eamonn Ceannt
National Photographic Archive, Meeting House Square, Temple Bar, Dublin 2.
Tel.: 01 6030371. Email: photoarchive@nli.ie

Celbridge Album
1990   160 photographs
Documentary pictures of Celbridge, Co. Kildare.
National Photographic Archive, Meeting House Square, Temple Bar, Dublin 2.
Tel.: 01 6030371. Email: photoarchive@nli.ie

Chandler, Edward C.
1855–1940   *c.*1,500 photographic prints, glass lantern slides, etc
Collection of studio portraits and other pictures assembled by the Chandler family.[8]
National Photographic Archive, Meeting House Square, Temple Bar, Dublin 2.
Tel.: 01 6030371. Email: photoarchive@nli.ie

Chapman, Robert L.
1880–1950
Photographs of streetscapes, landscapes and buildings taken in Dublin and surrounding counties.
Irish Picture Library, 69B Heather Road, Sandyford Industrial Estate, Dublin 18.
Tel.: 01 2950799. Email: ipl@fatherbrowne.com

Church of Ireland Archive Collection
Photographs of church buildings, clergy, laity and church plate.
Representative Church Body Library, Braemor Park, Churchtown, Dublin 14.
Tel.: 01 4923979. Email: library@ireland.anglican.org

Clare Railways Collection
1887–1961   *c.*300 photographs
Photographs taken by Leslie Hyland and Herbert Richards, mostly of the West Clare Railway.
Clare County Library, Mill Road, Ennis, Co. Clare.
Tel.: 065 6821616. Email: mailbox@clarelibrary.ie

Clarke, John Joseph
1897–1904   *c.*200 photographic prints
Pictures taken of people and buildings in the Westmoreland Street and St Stephen's Green area of Dublin while Clarke was a medical student there.
National Photographic Archive, Meeting House Square, Temple Bar, Dublin 2.
Tel.: 01 6030371. Email: photoarchive@nli.ie

---

8 Chandler, *Photography in Ireland, the nineteenth century*; idem, *Photography in Dublin in the Victorian era* (Dublin, 1980); idem & Peter Walsh, *Through the brass lidded eye* (Dublin, 1989).

Clonbrock Collection

1860–1930   *c.*3,900 glass negatives, lantern slides and photographic prints
Important big house photographs taken mostly on the Clonbrock estate in Co. Galway.
National Photographic Archive, Meeting House Square, Temple Bar, Dublin 2.
Tel.: 01 6030371. Email: photoarchive@nli.ie

Coghill, Sir Joscelyn

1865–1900   49 photographic copy prints
Pictures of Somerville and Coghill familes and of Drishane and Castletownshend in Co. Cork.
National Photographic Archive, Meeting House Square, Temple Bar, Dublin 2.
Tel.: 01 6030371. Email: photoarchive@nli.ie
More of his prints are to be found in the George Eastman House in New York and in the Getty Museum in Los Angeles.

Commissioners Of Irish Lights Collection

*c.*1900   500 glass plates, lantern slides and loose prints
Panoramic images taken by Sir Robert Ball around the coast of Ireland.
National Photographic Archive, Meeting House Square, Temple Bar, Dublin 2.
Tel.: 01 6030371. Email: photoarchive@nli.ie

Congested Districts Board

1906–14   120 photographic prints
Documentary photographs to supplement written reports on poor areas along the west coast.[9]
National Photographic Archive, Meeting House Square, Temple Bar, Dublin 2.
Tel.: 01 6030371. Email: photoarchive@nli.ie

Connemara Album

1892   43 images
Important documentary photographs taken in Connemara for James H. Tuke by Major Rutledge Fair who was an inspector with the Congested Districts Board.
National Photographic Archive, Meeting House Square, Temple Bar, Dublin 2.
Tel.: 01 6030371. Email: photoarchive@nli.ie

Convict Prisons Board Collection

1857–1927
Front and side mug shots of convicted prisoners.
National Archives, Bishop's Street, Dublin 8.
Tel.: 01 407 2300. Email: mail@nationalarchives.ie

---

9 E.E. Evans & Brian S. Turner, *Ireland's eye: the photographs of Robert John Welch* (Belfast, 1977); Morrissey (ed.), *On the verge of want*; Breathnach, *The Congested Districts Board of Ireland*.

Coolgreany Evictions Album
1887   46 photographic prints
Pictures taken at the fringes of evictions on the Brooke estate, Gorey in Co. Wexford.
National Photographic Archive, Meeting House Square, Temple Bar, Dublin 2.
Tel.: 01 6030371. Email: photoarchive@nli.ie

Cooper, H.F.
1908–61   *c.*200,000 glass plate negatives
Huge collection by this Strabane-based professional photographer depicting family,
political, sporting and cultural life in counties Tyrone and Donegal.
Public Records Office of Northern Ireland, 66 Balmoral Avenue, Belfast BT9 6NY.
Tel.: 028 90255905. Email: proni@dcalni.gov.uk

Cork Public Museum Collection
1870–2000
Miscellaneous photographs relating to Cork city and county.
Cork Public Museum, Fitzgerald Park, Cork.
Tel.: 021 4270679. Email: museum@corkcity.ie

Crawford Collection
1946   55 photographs
Interior and exterior images of the built environment in Kilkenny city.
Library Headquarters, 6 Rose Inn Street, Kilkenny.
Tel.: 056 7794160. Email: info@kilkennylibrary.ie

Curran, Michael J.
1901–39   239 positive and 12 negative images
Portraits of individuals and groups and other images of life in the Irish College in
Rome where the photographer was a student and later rector.
Archivista, Pontificio Collegio Irlandese, Via Santi Quattro 1, 00184 Roma.
Tel.: 0039 0677263408. Email: archives@irishcollege.org

Darkest Dublin Collection
1913   *c.*100 images
Documentary photographs of Dublin slums by John Cooke and others in the year
of the Dublin lock-out.
Royal Society of Antiquaries of Ireland, 63 Merrion Square, Dublin 2.
Tel.: 01 6761749. Email: rsai@rsai.ie

Davies, Michael
1952–59   185 copy prints.
Images by this England based photographer of trains, railway stations and other
shots relating to the Sligo-Leitrim and Cavan Leitrim narrow gauge railways.
Local Studies, Leitrim County Library, Ballinamore, Co. Leitrim.
Tel.: 071 9645567. Email: mconefrey@leitrimcoco.ie

Davitt, Michael

1879–82

Photographs of Michael Davitt and his Land League activities.

Michael Davitt National Memorial Museum, Land League Place, Straide, Foxford, Co. Mayo.

Tel.: 094 9031022. Email: davittmuseum@eircom.net

Day Collection

*c.*1890–1950   60 prints

Photographs taken by three generations of the Day family of buildings, streetscapes and people in Cork city.[10]

The Local Studies Department, Cork City Libraries, Grand Parade, Cork.

Tel.: 021 4924914. Email: localstudies_library@corkcity.ie

Deane, Thomas Manley

1886–1902   *c.*100 photographic prints

Photographs of public buildings in Dublin and Belfast which were designed by Deane.

National Photographic Archive, Meeting House Square, Temple Bar, Dublin 2.

Tel.: 01 6030371. Email: photoarchive@nli.ie

DeLacy Smyth, James

1864–1920 9 photographic prints and 6 photolithographic postcards

Mostly portraits of Irish political and church figures.

National Photographic Archive, Meeting House Square, Temple Bar, Dublin 2.

Tel.: 01 6030371. Email: photoarchive@nli.ie

Derry Collection

1860–1970   *c.*3,000 negatives

Images of Derry city and county and others of the north west of Ireland.[11]

Magee College Library, Northland Road, Derry, BT 487JL.

Tel.: 028 71375264. Email: illmagee@ulster.ac.uk

Diel, Roger and Sue,

Modern photographs of built environment, landscapes and streetscapes in Co. Clare.

Clare County Library, Mill Road, Ennis, Co. Clare.

Tel.: 065 6821616. Email: mailbox@clarelibrary.ie

---

10 Rynne & Wigham, *Forgotten Cork* and http://www.corkpastandpresent.ie; C. O'Corr, *Down memory lane: pictures of times past* (Cork, 1985); Tim Cadogan, *Cork in old photographs* (Dublin, 2003); Seán Radley, *Picture Millstreet: a photographic profile of Millstreet, 1880–1980* (Cork, 1997).   **11** Roy Hamilton, *100 years of Derry* (Belfast, 1999).

Diggin, Michael

1980–99   *c.*20 images
Pictures taken in Dublin, Aran Islands and Blasket Islands by this photographer from Tralee.[12]
National Photographic Archive, Meeting House Square, Temple Bar, Dublin 2.
Tel.: 01 6030371. Email: photoarchive@nli.ie

Dillon Album

1880–1920   19 photographic prints
Documentary pictures of horses and horse-racing in Ireland.
National Photographic Archive, Meeting House Square, Temple Bar, Dublin 2.
Tel.: 01 6030371. Email: photoarchive@nli.ie

Donegal Railways

1900–61
Collection of photographic prints of the various railway systems in Co. Donegal.[13]
Archives Service, Donegal County Council, Three Rivers Centre, Lifford, Co. Donegal.
Tel.: 074 9172490. Email: archivist@donegalcoco.ie

Doran, Hugh

1950–2000
Important collection of black-and-white photographs depicting the architecture of Dublin and many of the big houses throughout Ireland.[14]
The Irish Architectural Archive, 45 Merrion Square, Dublin 2.
Tel.: 01 6633040. Email: info@iarc.ie

Doyle, Colman

1954–2000   *c.* 28,000 prints and negatives.
Large and important collection covering events in Ireland by this *Irish Press* photographer.[15]
National Photographic Archive, Meeting House Square, Temple Bar, Dublin 2.
Tel.: 01 6030371. Email: photoarchive@nli.ie

Dripsey Woolen Mills

1925–26   113 photographic prints
Photographs of O'Shaughnessy family and their textile factory in Co. Cork.
National Photographic Archive, Meeting House Square, Temple Bar, Dublin 2.
Tel.: 01 6030371. Email: photoarchive@nli.ie

---

12 T.N. Biuso, 'Looking into Blasket Island photographs' in *Journal of Irish Studies*, 19, no. 4 (1984), 16–34.   **13** S. Flanders, *The County Donegal railway, an Irish railway pictorial* (London, 1996); E.M. Patterson, *The Lough Swilly railway* (Belfast, 1988); Seán Beattie, *Donegal: Ireland in old photographs* (Gloucester, 2004).   **14** See *Hugh Doran, photographer* (Dublin, 2007) (no author given) which was published by the Irish Architectural Archive.   **15** This collection is recently acquired and is still not available to researchers. See Colman Doyle, *All changed: fifty years of photographing Ireland* (Dublin, 2004). The text is by John Quinn.

Dublin Aerial Photographs

1960s
51 black and white aerial photographs taken by Photair Ltd.
48 black and white aerial photographs taken by Aerofilms Ltd.
526 colour aerial photographs by Denis McManus.
Dublin and Irish Local Studies Collections, Dublin City Library and Archive,
138–144 Pearse Street, Dublin 2.
Tel.: 01 6744999. Email: dublinstudies@dublincity.ie

Dublin County Collection

1942–44   215 images
Photographs taken for Irish Tourist Association in various parts of Co. Dublin.[16]
Dublin and Irish Local Studies Collections, Dublin City Library and Archive,
138–144 Pearse Street, Dublin 2.
Tel.: 01 6744999. Email: dublinstudies@dublincity.ie

Dublin Port Company Collection

Collection of photographs relating to activities in Dublin port.
Dublin Port Company, Port Centre, Alexandra Road, Dublin 1.
Tel.: 01 8550888. Email: dubport@dublin-port.ie

Duncan, Leland Lewis

1889–94   *c.*150 copy prints
Important documentary photographs of life at and near Annadale, Co. Leitrim.[17]
Irish Picture Library, 69B Heather Road, Sandyford Industrial Estate, Dublin 18.
Tel.: 01 2950799. Email: ipl@fatherbrowne.com. Copies of his 1889 photographs
are in the National Photographic Archives. See also Local Studies, Leitrim County
Library, Ballinamore, Co. Leitrim.
Tel.: 071 9645567. Email: mconefrey@leitrimcoco.ie

Eason Collection

1900–39   4,092 glass negatives
Picture postcards taken in different parts of Ireland.
National Photographic Archive, Meeting House Square, Temple Bar, Dublin 2.
Tel.: 01 6030371. Email: photoarchive@nli.ie

Easter Rising and Civil War

1916–23   *c.*200 photographic prints and postcards
Miscellaneous pictures of Dublin during the 1916 Rebellion and the Civil War.
National Photographic Archive, Meeting House Square, Temple Bar, Dublin 2.
Tel.: 01 6030371. Email: photoarchive@nli.ie

16 For other photographs of Dublin see E.E. O'Donnell, *The annals of Dublin fair city* (Dublin, 1987); Peter Pearson, *Between the mountains and the blue sea* (Dublin, 1998); idem, *Dublin city and citizens – a photographic celebration* (Dublin, 1988) produced by Dublin Camera club.   **17** Kelly, *The face of time.*

Eblana Collection
1870–90   *c.*2,900 glass negatives
Views of various cities, towns and rural areas in Ireland.
National Photographic Archive, Meeting House Square, Temple Bar, Dublin 2.
Tel.: 01 6030371. Email: photoarchive@nli.ie

Edgeworth, Kenneth
1870–1965   *c.*850 photographic prints, negatives and lantern slides
Photographs relating to the life of Lieut. Kenneth Edgeworth, Ballinalee, Co. Longford.
National Photographic Archive, Meeting House Square, Temple Bar, Dublin 2.
Tel.: 01 6030371. Email: photoarchive@nli.ie

Electricity Supply Board Collection
Photographs relating to the Rural Electrification Scheme and the history of the ESB.
Electricity Supply Board Archives, Parnell Avenue, Harold's Cross, Dublin 6.
Tel.: 01 6042132. Email: archive@esb.ie

Ellis Island Collection
1865–1925
Photographs of immigrants and of Ellis Island by Augustus Francis Sherman, Edwin Levick, Lewis W. Hine and other unknown photographers.
New York Public Library Digital Gallery. Images may be viewed and ordered on line.
See http://digitalgallery.nypl.org

Farnham Collection
1870–1960
*c.*500 photographs in albums and others separately framed; 50 glass negatives
Images of the Farnham family and estate at Cavan. Also some military photographs and one of Sir Edward Carson taken in 1912.[18]
Cavan County Museum, Virginia Road, Ballyjamesduff, Co. Cavan.
Tel.: 049 8544070. Email: ccmuseum@eircom.net

Fay, William G.
1915–50   40 photographic prints
Photographs of scenes and actors in films and play in which William Fay was involved.[19]
National Photographic Archive, Meeting House Square, Temple Bar, Dublin 2.
Tel.: 01 6030371. Email: photoarchive@nli.ie

Fenian Album
1865–70   26 photographic prints
A small *carte-de-visite* album depicting some prominent Fenians.
National Photographic Archive, Meeting House Square, Temple Bar, Dublin 2.
Tel.: 01 6030371. Email: photoarchive@nli.ie More of the Fenian photographs can be found at the National Archives, Bishop's Street, Dublin 8.
Tel.: 01 4072300. Email: mail@nationalarchives.ie

18 For more details see Brendan Scott, 'A catalogue of Farnham material held by Cavan County Museum' in *Breifne*, 4, no.42 (2006), pp 148–83.   **19** William G. Fay & Catherine Carswell, *The Fays of the Abbey Theatre: an autobiographical record* (London, 1935).

Fingal Postcard Collection

1900–60

Collection of picture postcards including some of Rush village, Rush Harbour and Kenure House.

Fingal County Library, County Hall, Swords, Co. Dublin.

Tel.: 01 8905000. Email: libs@fingalcoco.ie

Fitzelle Album

1922   33 photographic prints

Civil War pictures mostly in Dublin and Limerick

National Photographic Archive, Meeting House Square, Temple Bar, Dublin 2.

Tel.: 01 6030371. Email: photoarchive@nli.ie

Fitzherbert Photographs

1870–1910   10 photographic prints

Photographs relating to the Fitzherbert family of Blackcastle, Navan, Co. Meath.

Local Studies Department, Meath County Library, Railway Street, Navan, Co. Meath.

Tel.: 046 9021134. Email: ftallon@meathcoco.ie

Ford Factory Collection

1917–18   12 photographs

Photographs taken during construction of the Ford Factory in Cork.

The Local Studies Department, Cork City Libraries, Grand Parade, Cork.[20]

Tel.: 021 4924914. Email: localstudies_library@corkcity.ie

Gaelic Athletic Association Collection

1884–2007

Photographic collection relating to the GAA from its beginning to the present.

The Gaelic Athletic Association Museum, Croke Park, Dublin 3.

Tel.: 01 8558176. Email: gaamuseum@crokepark.ie

Gallagher, Fr Patrick

1940–80

Photographs relating to Donegal Historical Society and Co. Donegal.[21]

Archives Service, Donegal County Council, Three Rivers Centre, Lifford, Co. Donegal.

Tel.: 074 9172490. Email: archivist@donegalcoco.ie

---

20 Miriam Nyham, *Are you still below? The Ford marina plant, Cork, 1917–1984* (Cork, 2007). **21** Donald Martin, *Killybegs then and now* (Dublin, 1998).   **22** For photographs of Kinvara between 1880 and 1960 see C. Breatnach, *Kinvara: a seaport town on Galway bay* (Galway, 1997). Victor Whitmarsh, *Shadows on glass: Galway 1895–1960: a pictorial record* (Galway, 2003). For other more recent Galway photographs (1960–2000) see those taken by the *Connacht Tribune* photographer in Stan Shields, *Stan's Galway* (Dublin, 2006).

Galway Collection

1870–2000

Miscellaneous collection of photographs depicting images Galway city and county.[22]

Galway Local Archives, Library Headquarters, Island House, Cathedral Square, Galway.

Tel.: 091 562471. Email: info@galwaylibrary.ie

Garda Síochána Collection

1860–2000

Miscellaneous photographs relating to the Garda Síochána and earlier police forces in Ireland.

Garda Museum and Archives, Record Tower, Dublin Castle, Dublin 2.

Tel.: 01 6669998. Email: gatower@iol.ie

Godley, Anna

1880–1900   *c.*180 glass plates and prints

Some of the images were taken on and near the Killegar estate in Co. Leitrim and others were taken while travelling in Europe.

Local Studies, Leitrim County Library, Ballinamore, Co. Leitrim.

Tel.: 071 9645567. Email: mconefrey@leitrimcoco.ie

Green, Alice Stopford

1884–1945   18 photographic prints

Photographs relating to the life of Senator Alice Stopford Green, a native of Co. Meath.

National Photographic Archive, Meeting House Square, Temple Bar, Dublin 2.

Tel.: 01 6030371. Email: photoarchive@nli.ie

Green, William Alfred

1895–1935   4,114 glass plate negatives

Important photographic collection with pictures of Belfast, Co. Antrim and much of Ulster.

Ulster Folk and Transport Museum, Cultra, Hollywood, County Down, BT 18oEU.

Tel.: 028 90428428. Email: kenneth.anderson@nmni.com

Gribben, Thomas

1912–35   *c.*300 photographs

Good images of all aspects of life in and around Loughinisland, Co. Down.[23]

Down County Museum, The Mall, Downpatrick, Co. Down.

Tel.: 028 44615218. Email: lesley.simpson@downdc.gov.uk

---

23 For excellent photographs of Kilkeel and the Mourne district see Corr, *From the mountain to the sea.*

Guinness Collection

1880–2007   *c.*10,000 images
Photographs taken mostly at St James's Gate Brewery, though a small number were taken at breweries in Dundalk, Waterford, Kilkenny or offices in Cork, Ballinasloe and Limerick.
Guinness Archive, Guinness Storehouse, St James's Gate, Dublin 8.
Tel.: 01 4714557. Email: guinness.archives@diageo.com

Haffield Albums

1860–1930   *c.*850 photographic prints
Personal albums relating to the Haffield family, Kingstown and the Archer family of Louth.
National Photographic Archive, Meeting House Square, Temple Bar, Dublin 2.
Tel.: 01 6030371. Email: photoarchive@nli.ie

Hammond, Fred

1989   716 photographs
Photographic inventory of industrial archaeological sites in Co. Kilkenny.
Library Headquarters, 6 Rose Inn Street, Kilkenny.
Tel.: 056 7794160. Email: info@kilkennylibrary.ie

Hawarden, Lady Clementina

1859–64
Excellent early photographs taken on and near the Dundrum estate in Co. Tipperary by this Scottish-born though mostly London-based photographer.[24]
V & A Images, Victoria and Albert Museum, Cromwell Road, London, SW7 2RL.
Tel.: 020 79422479. Email: vanda.images@vam.ac.uk

Healy, James Augustine

1948–54   7 photographic prints
Pictures relate to the life of Healy who taught Irish literature at Colby College, in Maine.
National Photographic Archive, Meeting House Square, Temple Bar, Dublin 2.
Tel.: 01 6030371. Email: photoarchive@nli.ie

Hemphill, William Despard

1854–70   *c.*100 images
Important early and aesthetically pleasing photographs of Clonmel and surrounding areas of south Tipperary and north Waterford.[25]
South Tipperary County Museum, Clonmel, Co. Tipperary.
Tel.: 062 34551. Email: museum@southtippcoco.ie

---

24 Virginia Dodier, *Lady Clementina Hawarden: studies of life, 1857–1864* (London, 1999); Meyer, *Becoming: the photographs of Clementina Viscountess Hawarden.*   **25** Holland, *Tipperary images.*

Henderson, W.R.

1890–1920   *c.*300 glass plate negatives and 100 photographic prints
Views of towns and villages in Tyrone and Donegal by this Newtownstewart-based photographer.
Public Records Office of Northern Ireland, 66 Balmoral Avenue, Belfast BT9 6NY.
Tel.: 028 90255905. Email: proni@dcalni.gov.uk

Hickey, Des

1953–90   *c.*200 photographic prints
Pictures relating to the Wexford Festival, actors and writers.
National Photographic Archive, Meeting House Square, Temple Bar, Dublin 2.
Tel.: 01 6030371. Email: photoarchive@nli.ie

Hillery, Patrick

1965–89   *c.*3000 photographic prints, portraits and postcards
Mostly photographs taken during his time as President of Ireland and EEC Commissioner.
National Photographic Archive, Meeting House Square, Temple Bar, Dublin 2.
Tel.: 01 6030371. Email: photoarchive@nli.ie

Hinde, John

1957–72   497 colour postcards
Romanticized colourful views taken in various parts of Ireland.[26]
National Photographic Archive, Meeting House Square, Temple Bar, Dublin 2.
Tel.: 01 6030371. Email: photoarchive@nli.ie

Hogan, W.D.

1922   58 photographic prints
Images of Dublin during the months of June and July 1922.
National Photographic Archive, Meeting House Square, Temple Bar, Dublin 2.
Tel.: 01 6030371. Email: photoarchive@nli.ie

Hogg, Alexander

1888–1939   *c.*5,000 glass plate negatives and 1,500 lantern slides[27]
Important documentary images of Belfast, farming life and rural landscapes in Antrim.
Ulster Museum, Botanic Gardens, Belfast, BT9 5AB.
Tel.: 028 90383000. Email: vivienne.pollock.um@nics.gov.uk

Horgan, Jim

1954   49 glass lantern slides
Slides taken during the filming of *Moby Dick* near Youghal.
National Photographic Archive, Meeting House Square, Temple Bar, Dublin 2.
Tel.: 01 6030371. Email: photoarchive@nli.ie

26 *Hindesight: photographs and postcards by John Hinde Ltd, 1935–1971* (Dublin, 1993), published by the Irish Museum of Modern Art.   **27** Maguire, *Caught in time*.   **28** For more recent photographs of Kilkeel and Mourne district see Corr, *From the mountains to the sea.*

Howard, Paula & Hardiman, Nollag
1965–7   78 photographs
Colour streetscapes taken in and around Pearse Street, Dublin.
Irish Local Studies Collections, Dublin City Library and Archive, 138–144 Pearse Street, Dublin 2.
Tel.: 01 6744999. Email: dublinstudies@dublincity.ie

Hudson, Pat
1930–45   *c.*200 photographs
Photographs of local farmers and fishermen in Kilkeel and south Co. Down.[28]
Down County Museum, The Mall, Downpatrick, Co. Down.
Tel.: 028 44615218. Email: lesley.simpson@downdc.gov.uk

Hughes, Brian
1980–96   *c.*600 photographic prints
Documentary photographs of Belfast and Ulster.
National Photographic Archive, Meeting House Square, Temple Bar, Dublin 2.
Tel.: 01 6030371. Email: photoarchive@nli.ie

Hugh Lane Muncipal Gallery of Modern Art
1907–90
Collection of photographs relating to the Hugh Lane Gallery.
Hugh Lane Muncipal Gallery of Modern Art, Charlemont House, Parnell Square, Dublin 1.
Tel.: 01 8741903. Email: hughlane@iol.ie

Hulton Collection
1900–80   *c.*250 photographs
Some excellent images of life in Ireland which were taken by different photographers and collected by the London-based publisher Edward Hulton. The images may be viewed on line and purchased at www.gettyimages.com

Hyde, Douglas
1890s   66 photographs
Photographs of the Hyde family and neighbours at Frenchpark, Co. Roscommon.
James Hardiman Library, NUIG, University Road, Galway.
Tel.: 091 492540. Email: library@nuigalway.ie

Imperial War Museum Collection
1914–1945
An important photographic collection of soldiers who fought in the Irish regiments in both World Wars.[29]
Imperial War Museum, Visitor Room, All Saints Annexe, Austral Street,
London SE 11 48L.
Tel.: 0044 2074165333. Email: photos@iwm.org.uk

29 David Murphy, *Irish regiments in the world wars* (Oxford, 2007).

Invincibles Album
1882   47 photographic prints
Portraits of convicted criminals and other prisoners.
National Photographic Archive, Meeting House Square, Temple Bar, Dublin 2.
Tel.: 01 6030371. Email: photoarchive@nli.ie

Independent Newspapers Collection
1900–2000   *c.*300,000 images, glass plates, negatives and prints
Important and very large collection of news photography in Ireland in the twentieth
century.[30]
National Photographic Archive, Meeting House Square, Temple Bar, Dublin 2.
Tel.: 01 6030371. Email: photoarchive@nli.ie

Ireland, John de Courcy
1950–90   *c.*4,500 prints
Wide range of maritime related photographs by this maritime historian.
National Photographic Archive, Meeting House Square, Temple Bar, Dublin 2.
Tel.: 01 6030371. Email: photoarchive@nli.ie

Irish Architectural Archive Collection
1860–2000   *c.*300,000 photographs, slides and prints
Images of big houses, towns, streetscapes and built environment all over Ireland.
Irish Architectural Archive, 73 Merrion Square, Dublin 2.
Tel.: 01 6763430. Email: coriordan@iarc.ie

Irish Examiner Collection[31]
1900–2000
Photographs taken for this Cork newspaper during the twentieth century.[32]
The Irish Examiner, City Quarter, Lapps Quay, Cork.
Tel.: 021 4272722. Email: counter@examiner.ie

Irish Film Archive
1900–2000
Collection of photographic stills relating to Irish cinema.
Irish Film Archive, Film Institute of Ireland, 6 Eustace Street, Dublin 2.
Tel.: 01 6795744. Email: archive@ifc.ie

Irish Linen Centre Collection
Photographic collection relating to the linen industry in Ireland.
Irish Linen Centre & Lisburn Museum, Market Square, Lisburn, BT28 1AG.
Tel.: 028 92663377. Email: irishlinencentre@lisburn.gov.uk

30 The pre-1930 images have been catalogued and are available on the on-line catalogue.
Negatives relating to Northern Ireland between 1967 and 1978 are also available. The
cataloguing of this large collection is ongoing and all the images will not be available to
researchers until this work is completed.   **31** Formerly the *Cork Examiner*.   **32** Some of
these photographs have been published in Stephen Coughlan (ed.), *Picture that: a century of
Cork memories* (Cork, 1986); S. Coughlan (ed.), *Picture that again* (Cork, 1986). The other

Irish Rugby Football Union
1874–2007
Collection of photographs relating to rugby in Ireland.
Irish Rugby Football Union, 62 Landsdowne Road, Dublin 4.
Tel.: 01 6684601. Email: info@irishrugby.ie

Irish Theatre Collection
Collection of photographs relating to theatres, amateur groups and theatre clubs.
Irish Theatre Archive, City Assembly House, 58 South William Street, Dublin 2.
Tel.: 01 6775877. Email: cityarchives@dublincity.ie

The Irish Times Collection
1900–2007   *c.*182,000 images in black and white and colour
Most of the images are by *Irish Times* photographers and are relatively recent ones, though some are from the early 1900s.
Many images in the collection may be accessed and ordered on line at http://www.ireland.com/photosales

Irish Traditional Music Collection
*c.*3,000 images
Photographs relating to traditional Irish musicians and events.
Irish Traditional Music Archive, 63 Merrion Square, Dublin 2.
Tel.: 01 6619699. Email: info@itma.ie

Jackson, Dean Wyse
1948   85 photographic prints
Photographs of archaeology, architecture and topography of Cashel, Co. Tipperary.
National Photographic Archive, Meeting House Square, Temple Bar, Dublin 2.
Tel.: 01 6030371. Email: photoarchive@nli.ie

Johnson, Nevill
1952–3
Photographic record of Dublin by the English artist and photographer.
RTÉ Stills Library. For information and to order see
http://www.rte.ie/laweb/ll/ll_stills.html

Joly, John
1890–1900   306 lantern slides and colour screens
Joly's slides are interesting because of his early experimentation with colour photography.[33]
National Photographic Archive, Meeting House Square, Temple Bar, Dublin 2.
Tel.: 01 6030371. Email: photoarchive@nli.ie

Cork Newspaper, the *Evening Echo*, has published some of its photographs in *Echoes of the past: a trip down memory lane* (Cork, 2001) and *Echoes of the past: where we sported and played* (Cork, 2005).   **33** Stephen Coonan, 'The discovery and evolution of single-image additive colour photography' (M. Lit. thesis, Trinity College Dublin, 1995).

Kahn, Albert
1913   *c.*100 autochrome colour prints
Excellent documentary pictures taken in Galway, Offaly, Wicklow and Louth by
Marguerite Mespoulet and Madeleine Mignon–Alba for Albert Kahn's 'Archives of
the planet' collection.[34]
Albert Kahn Museum, 14 Rue du Port, Boulogne-Billancourt, Paris.
Tel.: +33(0)15519 2800. Email: museealbertkahn@cg92.fr

Kane, Aloysius
1950–75   178 black-and-white photographs
Images of Dublin city streetscapes, buildings, trams, docks and railways.
Dublin and Irish Local Studies Collections, Dublin City Library and Archive,
138–144 Pearse Street, Dublin 2.
Tel.: 01 6744999. Email: dublinstudies@dublincity.ie

Kenny Collection
1870–1980   *c.* 20,000 photographic images
Images of people, places, historic and sporting events and many other aspects of life
in Galway city.
The Kenny Gallery, High Street & Middle Street, Galway.
Tel.: 091 534760. Email: tomk@kennys.ie

Keogh Collection
1914–50   232 glass negatives
Negatives of 1916 Rising, Civil War and portraits of some of the key personalities.
National Photographic Archive, Meeting House Square, Temple Bar, Dublin 2.
Tel.: 01 6030371. Email: photoarchive@nli.ie

Kernoff, Harry
1912–70   45 photographic prints.
Pictures related to aspects of the life of the artist and painter Harry Kernoff.
National Photographic Archive, Meeting House Square, Temple Bar, Dublin 2.
Tel.: 01 6030371. Email: photoarchive@nli.ie

Kerry Postcard Collection
1894–1960
Collection of picture postcards taken by various photographers in Co. Kerry.[35]
Kerry County Library, Moyderwell, Tralee, Co. Kerry.
Tel.: 066 7121200. Email: localhistory@kerrycolib.ie

Kildare Collection
1890–2000
Copies of the Lawrence collection and other miscellaneous photographs relating
to Co. Kildare.
Kildare Library and Arts Service, Main Street, Newbridge, Co. Kildare.
Tel.: 045 431109. Email: colibrary@kildarecoco.ie

34 Lorna Siggins, 'Peaceful pictures on eve of war' in the *Irish Times*, 19 June 2007.   **35** Some

Kilgannon, Tadhg
1900–10   55 photographs
Photographs of buildings, streetscapes, people and shop fronts in Co. Sligo.
Local Studies Collection, Sligo County Library, Westward Centre, Bridge Street,
Sligo. Tel.: 071 9111854. Email: sligolib@sligococo.ie

Kilkenny Architectural Collection
1946   107 photographic prints and negatives
Pictures of Kilkenny City streetscapes and built environment in June 1946.
National Photographic Archive, Meeting House Square, Temple Bar, Dublin 2.
Tel.: 01 6030371. Email: photoarchive@nli.ie

Kilkenny City Collection
1968–72   178 photographs
Photographs of streetscapes in Kilkenny city by Bolton Street students.
Library Headquarters, 6 Rose Inn Street, Kilkenny.
Tel.: 056 7794160. Email: info@kilkennylibrary.ie

Kilronan Albums
1858   106 photographic prints and negatives
Early calotype and salt prints, mostly of built environment by members of the
Tenison family from Kilronan, Co. Roscommon.
National Photographic Archive, Meeting House Square, Temple Bar, Dublin 2.
Tel.: 01 6030371. Email: photoarchive@nli.ie

Lawrence Family Album
1850–1900
Portraits of the Lawrence family and images of Lisreaghan House and Lawrencetown
village in Co. Galway.[36]
Galway Local Archives, Library Headquarters, Island House, Cathedral Square, Galway.
Tel.: 091 562471. Email: info@galwaylibrary.ie

Lawrence, William
1865–1914   40,000 glass negatives and *c.*15,000 photographic prints
Important images either gathered or commissioned by Lawrence covering most of
Ireland.[37]
National Photographic Archive, Meeting House Square, Temple Bar, Dublin 2.
Tel.: 01 6030371. Email: photoarchive@nli.ie

Lawrence Photographic Project Collection
1990   1019 photographic colour prints and negatives
Modern views corresponding to some of those in the original Lawrence compilation.
National Photographic Archive, Meeting House Square, Temple Bar, Dublin 2.
Tel.: 01 6030371. Email: photoarchive@nli.ie

of these images are to be found on http://askaboutireland.ie   **36** These photographs may
be viewed on line at http://www.askaboutireland.ie   **37** Hickey, *The light of other days*;

Leitrim County Collection

1870–2000

Miscellaneous photographs relating Co. Leitrim including photographs taken by Leland L. Duncan, Fr Browne and 28 prints taken in 1983 during the search for the kidnapped Don Tidey.

Local Studies, Leitrim County Library, Ballinamore, Co. Leitrim.

Tel.: 071 9645567. Email: mconefrey@leitrimcoco.ie

Levingston Collection

1893–4.   50 glass lanterns

Images of people and places in Galway, Dublin and Kilkee, Co. Clare.

National Photographic Archive, Meeting House Square, Temple Bar, Dublin 2.

Tel.: 01 6030371. Email: photoarchive@nli.ie

Limerick County Collection

*c.*1965   *c.*400 photographs

Aerial photographs of Co. Limerick which were used by Limerick County Council.[38]

Limerick Studies Department, Limerick County Library HQ, 58 O'Connell Street, Limerick.

Tel.: 061 496529. Email: tstoran@limerickcoco.ie

Longford County Collection

1890–2000

Lawrence collection on microfilm and other miscellaneous photographs relating to Co. Longford.

Longford County Library, Town Centre, Longford.

Tel.: 043 41124. Email: library@longfordcoco.ie

Lucas, Ralph & Lynch, P.J.

1943–4   *c.*200 black-and-white photographs

These archaeologists took photographs of places of historical interest in Limerick city and county for the Irish Tourist Association.

Limerick Studies Department, Limerick County Library HQ, 58 O'Connell Street, Limerick.

Tel.: 061 496529. Email: tstoran@limerickcoco.ie

Luftwaffe Collection

1940   16 copy prints

Aerial photographs of Dublin taken by the German Luftwaffe on 29 December 1940.

National Photographic Archive, Meeting House Square, Temple Bar, Dublin 2.

Tel.: 01 6030371. Email: photoarchive@nli.ie

Chandler & Walsh, *Through the brass lidded eye.*   **38** The *Limerick Leader* newspaper has a photographic archive. See the six volumes by Seán Curtin called *Limerick: a stroll down memory lane* which have been published between 2002 and 2006.

MacConnoran, Michael

1922   17 photographic copy prints
Pictures by an amateur photographer taken in Dublin in 1922.
National Photographic Archive, Meeting House Square, Temple Bar, Dublin 2.
Tel.: 01 6030371. Email: photoarchive@nli.ie

MacNamara, George U.

*c.*1910
Images of archaeological sites in Co. Clare.
Clare County Library, Mill Road, Ennis, Co. Clare.
Tel.: 065 6821616. Email: mailbox@clarelibrary.ie

Malone, Eric V.

1950–70   *c.*500 photographs
Images of people and buildings taken in Downpatrick and surrounding areas in Co.
Down.
Down County Museum, The Mall, Downpatrick, Co. Down.
Tel.: 028 44615218. Email: lesley.simpson@downdc.gov.uk

Mason Collection

1890–1900   *c.*2,300 glass lantern slides
Wide range of images, some of which are photographic images, used as aids in
teaching Irish history.
National Photographic Archive, Meeting House Square, Temple Bar, Dublin 2.
Tel.: 01 6030371. Email: photoarchive@nli.ie

McKeown, Roy

2002–3   *c.*80 photographs
Aerial photographs taken in the Ballymena area of Co. Antrim.
NEELB Local Studies Department, Ballymena Central Library, 5 Pat's Brae,
Ballymena, BT43 5AX.
Tel.: 028 2563 3960. Email: michael.lynn@ni-libraries.net

McKinney, William Fee

1885–1910   *c.*600 glass negatives
Excellent photographs of people, buildings and farm implements in rural south
Antrim.
Ulster Folk and Transport Museum, Cultra, Hollywood, Co. Down, BT 180EU.
Tel.: 028–9042 8428. Email: tkenneth.anderson@talk21.com
or Sentry Hill, 40 Ballycraigy Road, Newtownabbey, Co. Down. BT36 8SK.
Tel.: 028 90832363. Email: sentry.hill@btconnect.com

McNamara, Christy

1990 onwards
Excellent, mostly black-and-white photographs, especially of Irish musicians.
Durra cottage, Barefield, Ennis, Co. Clare.
Tel.: 086 8119058. Email: Christy.mcnamara@hotmail.com

McNeill, Daniel J.

1950–85   *c.*20,000

Images of people, buildings and events in Downpatrick and much of Co. Down.
Down County Museum, The Mall, Downpatrick, County Down.
Tel.: 028 4461 5218. Email: lesley.simpson@downdc.gov.uk

Meath Collection

1870–2000   *c.*300 photographs and postcards

Images of towns, streetscapes and buildings of Co. Meath. Also some aerial
photographs taken in Meath.
Local Studies Department, Meath County Library, Railway Street, Navan, Co. Meath.
Tel.: 046 9021134. Email: ftallon@meathcoco.ie

Medieval Tomb Sculptures

Monochrome negatives.
Modern photographs by David Davison of medieval tomb sculptures in Ireland.
Irish Picture Library, 69B Heather Road, Sandyford Industrial Estate, Dublin 18.
Tel.: 01 2950799. Email: ipl@fatherbrowne.com

Morgan, Alexander Campbell

1954–7   2,831 film negatives

Medium- and low-level aerial pictures taken in most parts of Ireland.
National Photographic Archive, Meeting House Square, Temple Bar, Dublin 2.
Tel.: 01 6030371. Email: photoarchive@nli.ie

Mountjoy Prison Portraits

1857 and 1866   150 salt and albumen photographs

Mug shots of Mountjoy prisoners (including Jeremiah O'Donovan Rossa) taken in
August 1857 and November 1866.[39]
New York Public Library Digital Gallery. Images may be viewed and ordered on line.
See http://digitalgallery.nypl.org

Mulcahy, Richard

1906–65   *c.*300 photographic prints and negatives

Mostly photographs of General Richard Mulcahy's family. Includes one of Michael
Collin's funeral.
National Photographic Archive, Meeting House Square, Temple Bar, Dublin 2.
Tel.: 01 6030371. Email: photoarchive@nli.ie

Mullingar Collection

1900–2000

Miscellaneous photographs relating to Mullingar and surrounding areas.[40]
Westmeath County Library HQ, Dublin Road, Mullingar, Co. Westmeath.
Tel.: 044 40781. Email: library@westmeathcoco.ie

---

39 The albums belonged to Thomas Aiskew Larcom (1801–79). See Thomas E. Jordan, *An imaginative empiricist – Thomas Aiskew Larcom (1801–1879) and Victorian Ireland* (Dublin, 2002).
40 Matt Nolan, *Mullingar: just for the record* (Dublin, 1999).

Murtagh Collection

1900–40

Images of such events as the 1916 Rising, burning of Cork city and 1932 Eucharistic Congress.

RTÉ Stills Library. For information and to order see
http://www.rte.ie/laweb/ll/ll_stills.html

National Maritime Museum Collection

Photographic collection relating to maritime history of Ireland.

National Maritime Museum of Ireland, Haigh Terrace, Dun Laoghaire, Co. Dublin. Tel.: 01 2800969.

Nelson, Francis

*c.*1900   64 photographs

Pictures of scenic views together with exterior and interior shots of important buildings in Co. Sligo.

Local Studies Collection, Sligo County Library, Westward Centre, Bridge Street, Sligo. Tel.: 071 9111854. Email: sligolib@sligococo.ie

O'Brennan, Kathleen,

1916–30   92 photographic prints

Mostly about personal life of the journalist and republican Kathleen O'Brennan.

National Photographic Archive, Meeting House Square, Temple Bar, Dublin 2. Tel.: 01 6030371. Email: photoarchive@nli.ie

O'Connor, Alan

1990–95   *c.*200 photographic prints and 400 film negatives

Images depicting the cultural diversity of Dublin in the 1990s.[41]

National Photographic Archive, Meeting House Square, Temple Bar, Dublin 2. Tel.: 01 6030371. Email: photoarchive@nli.ie

O'Connor, Fergus

1890–1915   *c.*600 glass negatives

These images of places and activities were taken mostly in the cities and towns of Ireland.

National Photographic Archive, Meeting House Square, Temple Bar, Dublin 2. Tel.: 01 6030371. Email: photoarchive@nli.ie

O'Connor, Larry

1870–1910   115 photographs

Images of Dublin city and county

Dublin and Irish Local Studies Collections, Dublin City Library and Archive, 138–144 Pearse Street, Dublin 2. Tel.: 01 6744999. Email: dublinstudies@dublincity.ie

---

41 Colm Lincoln, *Dublin as a work of art* (Dublin, 1992).

O'Dea, John P.

1937–66   *c.*4,200 photographic prints and negatives
Important collection which documents rail transport in Ireland over thirty year period.
National Photographic Archive, Meeting House Square, Temple Bar, Dublin 2.
Tel.: 01 6030371. Email: photoarchive@nli.ie

O'Dowda, Dermot

1982–91   27 photographic prints
Mostly colour prints of life in Donegal, Kerry and Cork.
National Photographic Archive, Meeting House Square, Temple Bar, Dublin 2.
Tel.: 01 6030371. Email: photoarchive@nli.ie

O'Neill, J.W.

1916   29 photographic prints
Images of interior and exterior of the General Post Office after the 1916 Rising.
National Photographic Archive, Meeting House Square, Temple Bar, Dublin 2.
Tel.: 01 6030371. Email: photoarchive@nli.ie

Ordnance Survey of Ireland

1970–2000
Large collection of aerial photographs taken at different altitudes covering all of the Republic of Ireland. Some images are in black and white and others in colour.
Ordnance Survey of Ireland, Phoenix Park, Dublin 8.
Tel.: 01 8025307. Email: photosales@osi.ie

Ordnance Survey of Northern Ireland

1959–2007   *c.*500,000 aerial photographs
Black and white and colour aerial photographs, mostly medium to low altitude, of all parts of Northern Ireland.
Ordnance Survey of Northern Ireland, Colby House, Stranmillis Court, Malone Lower, Belfast BT9 5BJ.
Tel.: 028 90255755. Email: osni@osni.gov.uk

Our Own Place Collection

1993–95   700 colour prints
Pictorial survey of Ireland taken mostly by members of the Federation of Local History Societies.
National Photographic Archive, Meeting House Square, Temple Bar, Dublin 2.
Tel.: 01 6030371. Email: photoarchive@nli.ie

Panoramic Photographic Albums

1905–08   514 photographic prints
Panoramic views taken, from both land and sea, around Ireland's coastline.
National Photographic Archive, Meeting House Square, Temple Bar, Dublin 2.
Tel.: 01 6030371. Email: photoarchive@nli.ie

Patrick Pearse Collection

1900–16
Photographs relating to Patrick Pearse and St Enda's school.
Pearse Museum, St Enda's Park, Rathfarnham, Dublin 14.
Tel.: 01 4934208. Email: kilmainhamgaol@opw.ie

Pontificio Collegio Irlandese Collection

1890–2007
Miscellaneous photographs relating to life in the Irish College in Rome.
Archivista, Pontificio Collegio Irlandese, Via Santi Quattro 1, 00184 Roma.
Tel.: 0039 0677263408. Email: archives@irishcollege.org

Poole, A.H.

1884–1954   c.65,000 glass negatives and accompanying note books
Images of people and events in Waterford, Wexford and southern Kilkenny.[42]
National Photographic Archive, Meeting House Square, Temple Bar, Dublin 2.
Tel.: 01 6030371. Email: photoarchive@nli.ie

Poulaphuca Collection

1939
Images of houses and bridges and other items relating to the flooding of the reservoir.
Royal Society of Antiquaries of Ireland, 63 Merrion Square, Dublin 2.
Tel.: 01 6761749. Email: rsai@rsai.ie

Power, Rosemary

1960s   c.300 colour prints
Photographs of people and events by this Cavan-based professional photographer.
Johnston Central Library and Farnham Centre, Farnham Street, Cavan.
Tel.: 049 4378500. Email: b.connolly@cavancoco.ie

Price, Dorothy

1910–25   11 photographic prints and 9 negatives
Images of Dorothy Stopford Price and her colleagues in the Meath Hospital.
National Photographic Archive, Meeting House Square, Temple Bar, Dublin 2.
Tel.: 01 6030371. Email: photoarchive@nli.ie

Quane, Dr Michael

1920–65   48 photographic prints
Images relate to his work with the Department of Education and some endowed schools.
National Photographic Archive, Meeting House Square, Temple Bar, Dublin 2.
Tel.: 01 6030371. Email: photoarchive@nli.ie

---

42 Griffin, *A parcel from the past: Waterford as seldom seen before*; C. Lincoln, 'First photographs of Ardmore?' in *Ardmore Journal*, 5 (1988), pp 36–9.

Hooker O'Malley Roelofs, Helen

1974–95   434 photographic prints
Mostly views, detail of ancient monastic sites in Ireland and informal portraits.
National Photographic Archive, Meeting House Square, Temple Bar, Dublin 2.
Tel.: 01 6030371. Email: photoarchive@nli.ie

Ritchie-Pickow Collection

1952–3   *c.*1,887 photographs
Important documentary photographs taken by the American couple George Pickow
and Jean Ritchie who had an interest in folklore and traditional Irish music.
James Hardiman Library, National University of Ireland, Galway.
Tel.: 091 524411 ext. 3636. Email: kieran@sulacco.library.ucg.ie

Roscommon Collection

Miscellaneous collection of photographs relating to Co. Roscommon.
Roscommon County Library, Library Buildings, Abbey Street, Roscommon.
Tel.: 090 6637271. Email: roslib@eircom.net

Royal Archives, Windsor Castle

1860–80   77 copy prints
Copies of photographs of scenic views and public buildings in Ireland.
National Photographic Archive, Meeting House Square, Temple Bar, Dublin 2.
Tel.: 01 6030371. Email: photoarchive@nli.ie

Royal Dublin Society

Miscellaneous photographs relating to the Royal Dublin Society.
Royal Dublin Society, Merrion Road, Ballsbridge, Dublin 4.
Tel.: 01 6680866. Ext. 386. Email: info@rds.ie

Royal Irish Constabulary

220 photographs
Images relating to the Royal Irish Constabulary.[43]
Trinity College Library, College Street, Dublin 2.
Tel.: 01 8961661.

Royal Society of Antiquaries of Ireland

1870–2000   *c.*20,000 prints, lantern slides and negatives
Images of archaeological sites and historic buildings throughout Ireland.
Royal Society of Antiquaries of Ireland, 63 Merrion Square, Dublin 2.
Tel.: 01 6761749. Email: rsai@rsai.ie

Royal Ulster Rifles Regimental Museum

1900–50
Photographic albums relating to the Royal Ulster Rifles regiment.
RHQ The Royal Irish Rangers, 5 Waring Street, Belfast BT 12EW.
Tel.: 028 90232086.

43 Jim Herlihy, *The Royal Irish Constabulary: a short history and genealogical guide* (Dublin, 1997).

RTÉ Guide Collection

1961–81

Images of presenters, staff and guests of radio and television programmes.[44]

RTÉ Stills Library. For information and to order see

http://www.rte.ie/laweb/ll/ll_stills.html

RTÉ Stills Department Collection

1961–2001

Negatives and slides of television and radio personalities and guests.[45]

RTÉ Stills Library. For information and to order see

http://www.rte.ie/laweb/ll/ll_stills.html

RTÉ Stills Library Collection

1900–2000

These are important images, especially good for the period 1916–23, acquired from a variety of sources for television programmes.[46]

RTÉ Stills Library. For information and to order see http://www.rte.ie/laweb/ll/ ll_stills.html

Scully, Vincent

1885–1925   15 photographic prints

Images of Scully family at their house at Golden, Co. Tipperary.

National Photographic Archive, Meeting House Square, Temple Bar, Dublin 2.

Tel.: 01 6030371. Email: photoarchive@nli.ie

Schorman, Sonia

1990s   *c*.2,500 photographs

The photographs are of sites of historical and archaeological interest in Co. Clare.

Clare County Library, Mill Road, Ennis, Co. Clare.

Tel.: 065 6821616. Email: mailbox@clarelibrary.ie

SEELB Collection

1880–1920

Prints from Lawrence and Welch collections and other photographs relating to Co. Antrim and Co. Down.

Local Studies Unit, SEELB, Library Headquarters, Ballynahinch, Co. Down, BT24 8DH.

Tel.: 028 97566437. Email: mary.bradley@ni-libraries.net

---

44 Most of these photographs were taken by Roy Bedell, the RTÉ Guide staff photographer.   **45** *RTÉ Off camera: images from the early years of RTÉ television* (Dublin, 2004). No author or editor given, introduction by Gay Byrne.   **46** For examples of the 1916–23 photographs in the collection see Louise Jefferson, *Dublin then and now: scenes from a revolutionary city* (Belfast, 2006).

Shackleton, Jane Wigham

1890–1908

Images of Irish waterways, Aran Islands and many taken around Ireland while on excursions with the Royal Society of Antiquaries of Ireland.[47]

Royal Society of Antiquaries of Ireland, 63 Merrion Square, Dublin 2.

Tel.: 01 6761749. Email: rsai@rsai.ie

Shard Collection

1895–1905

Images from south Dublin and north Wicklow.

RTÉ Stills Library. For information and to order see

http://www.rte.ie/laweb/ll/ll_stills.html

Shaw, Rose

1905–23   30 photographs

Excellent aesthetically pleasing pictures of life in Clogher Valley, Co. Tyrone.[48]

Ulster Folk and Transport Museum, Cultra, Hollywood, Co. Down, BT 18oEU.

Tel.: 028 9042 8428. Email: kenneth.anderson@nmni.com

Sheehy Skeffington, Hanna

1885–1956   *c.*400 photographic prints

Mostly portraits of Hanna Sheehy Skeffington, her family, colleagues and friends.

National Photographic Archive, Meeting House Square, Temple Bar, Dublin 2.

Tel.: 01 6030371. Email: photoarchive@nli.ie

Sligo Landed Gentry

1880–1920   52 portraits

An album containing portraits of landed gentry in Co. Sligo.

Local Studies Collection, Sligo County Library, Westward Centre, Bridge Street, Sligo. Tel.: 071 9111854. Email: sligolib@sligococo.ie

Smith, John Shaw

1845–55   *c.*360 calotype negatives

Most of this collection were taken outside Ireland, though there are some important early photographs of such places as Glendalough, Monasterboice, Powerscourt and Rostrevor.

George Eastman House, International Museum of Photography and Film, Rochester, New York. Photographs may be viewed and ordered on line at http://www. eastmanhouse.org

---

47 I am indebted to Chris Corlett for the information on this collection and several other collections held by the Royal Society of Antiquaries of Ireland.   **48** Rose Shaw, *Carleton's country* (Dublin, 1930).

Somerville Collection

1870s   36 photographs
Images of people and buildings in Co. Sligo.
Local Studies Collection, Sligo County Library, Westward Centre, Bridge Street, Sligo. Tel.: 071 9111854. Email: sligolib@sligococo.ie

Spillane Collection

1890–1913   26 glass negatives
Images of people and events in Castletownbeare, Co. Cork.
National Photographic Archive, Meeting House Square, Temple Bar, Dublin 2.
Tel.: 01 6030371. Email: photoarchive@nli.ie

St Kieran's College, Kilkenny

1850–2000
Miscellaneous photographs relating to St Kieran's secondary school and seminary.
St Kieran's College, Kilkenny.
Tel.: 056 21086. Email: skc1782@iol.ie

Stereo Pairs Collection

1860–83   3,059 glass negatives
Stereoscopic images of scenic views taken in 26 different counties.[49]
National Photographic Archive, Meeting House Square, Temple Bar, Dublin 2.
Tel.: 01 6030371. Email: photoarchive@nli.ie

Stokes, Dorothy

1920–65   *c.*800 prints
Photographs taken in various parts of Ireland by this South African-born woman who taught in the Dublin Royal Irish Academy of Music.
National Photographic Archive, Meeting House Square, Temple Bar, Dublin 2.
Tel.: 01 6030371. Email: photoarchive@nli.ie

Taggart, Maurice

1950–95   *c.*90 photographs
Photographs taken in the Carrickfergus area of Co. Antrim.
NEELB Local Studies Department, Ballymena Central Library, 5 Pat's Brae, Ballymena, BT43 5AX.
Tel.: 028 2563 3960. Email: michael.lynn@ni-libraries.net

Tempest Collection

1904–10   91 glass negatives
Pictures of Dundalk, Ardee and surrounding areas by Harry Tempest.
National Photographic Archive, Meeting House Square, Temple Bar, Dublin 2.
Tel.: 01 6030371. Email: photoarchive@nli.ie

49 National Gallery of Ireland, *Ireland 1860–80: from stereo photographs* (Dublin, 1982).

Ternan, Alfred R.W.

1880–1960   *c.*500 colour film slides and 8 glass negatives
Most of these images date from 1930–60 and were taken in Dublin by this architect.
National Photographic Archive, Meeting House Square, Temple Bar, Dublin 2.
Tel.: 01 6030371. Email: photoarchive@nli.ie

Therman, Dorothy Harrison

1981–91   144 photographic prints and 104 colour film slides
Colour prints of people and places on Tory Island, Co. Donegal.[50]
National Photographic Archive, Meeting House Square, Temple Bar, Dublin 2.
Tel.: 01 6030371. Email: photoarchive@nli.ie

Thornton, Col. F.

1929–33   241 photographic prints
Mostly personal photographs by this First World War British army officer.
National Photographic Archive, Meeting House Square, Temple Bar, Dublin 2.
Tel.: 01 6030371. Email: photoarchive@nli.ie

Thurles Collection

1985–2000   200 photographs
Views of town, buildings, streets and people taken by Thurles Camera Club.
Tipperary Studies, Cathedral Street, Thurles, Co. Tipperary.[51]
Tel.: 0504 29278. Email: studies@tipperarylibraries.ie

Tilbrook, Richard

1960–75   71 colour slides
Good documentary photographs of Dublin city centre and rural Ireland before
rapid change set in.
National Photographic Archive, Meeting House Square, Temple Bar, Dublin 2.
Tel.: 01 6030371. Email: photoarchive@nli.ie

Tuke, James H.

1892   46 photographs in a single album
Important documentary photographs taken in Conemara by Robert Rutledge-Fair
for the philanthropist James H. Tuke.[52]
National Photographic Archive, Meeting House Square, Temple Bar, Dublin 2.
Tel.: 01 6030371. Email: photoarchive@nli.ie

Tyers, Padraig

1888–1960   *c.*110 photographic prints
Copies of original images of life in Dingle peninsula collected by Tyers.[53]
National Photographic Archive, Meeting House Square, Temple Bar, Dublin 2.
Tel.: 01 6030371. Email: photoarchive@nli.ie

---

50 Dorothy Harrison Therman, *Stories from Tory Island* (Dublin, 1989).   **51** Tipperary Studies
Library in Thurles also has a large collection of miscellaneous photographs relating to County
Tipperary, including photographs of Holy Cross, civil war images and King Edward's 1904 visit
to Clogheen.   **52** Sara Smyth, 'Tuke's Connemara Album' in Breathnach, *Framing the west*, pp
29–47.   **53** Padraig Tyers, *Ceanara Chorca Dhuibhne: Cnuasach Grianfraf, 1888–1960* (Dún

Ulster Museum Collection

1850–1950   144 photographic copy prints
Copies of original portraits of well-known Irish people.
National Photographic Archive, Meeting House Square, Temple Bar, Dublin 2.
Tel.: 01 6030371. Email: photoarchive@nli.ie

University College Cork Collection

1850 onwards
Collection of photographs documenting the growth and development of the college.
National University of Ireland, Cork College Archive, University Heritage Office,
University College, Cork.
Tel.: 021 903552. Email: v.teehan@ucc.ie

University College Dublin Folklore Department

1890–2000   *c.* 70,000 images, prints, glass plates, negatives and colour slides
Photographs taken in Ireland, mostly though not exclusively along the west coast,
to supplement the folklore gathered there.
University College Dublin Delargy Centre for Irish Folklore, Belfield, Dublin 4.
Tel.: 01 7068216. Email: emer.nicheallaigh@ucd.ie

Valentine Collection

1903–60   *c.*3,000 glass negatives and film negatives
Commercial postcard images of towns, villages and public buildings in Ireland.[54]
National Photographic Archive, Meeting House Square, Temple Bar, Dublin 2.
Tel.: 01 6030371. Email: photoarchive@nli.ie

Waterford City Archives

1870–1990   *c.*5,000 photographic prints
Miscellaneous photographs relating to Waterford.
Waterford City Archives, City Hall, The Mall, Waterford.
Tel.: 051 843123. Email: archives@waterfordcorp.ie

Welch, Robert J.

1885–1935   *c.*10,000 negatives and prints
Excellent documentary images of industrialized Belfast, Ulster and much of Ireland.
Approximately 8,000 Harland & Wolff images[55] are in the Ulster Folk and Transport
Museum, Cultra, Hollywood, Co. Down, BT 180EU.
Tel.: 028 9042 8428. Email: uftmphotoarchive@talk21.com More of his
photographs are in the Ulster Museum, Botanic Gardens, Belfast, BT9 5AB.
Tel.: 028 9038 3000. See http://www.ulstermuseum.org.uk 400 of his photographs
are in the Sir Benjamin Stone Collection in Birmingham Central Library[56],
Chamberlain Square, Birmingham, B3 3HQ.
Tel.: 0121 303 4511. Email: central.library@birmingham.gov.uk

Chaoin, 1991).   **54** Robert Smart, 'James Valentine, 1859–1879' in Martin Kemp (ed.),
Masterworks of photography from the University of St Andrews (Edinburgh, 1996).   **55** Michael
McCaughan, *Steel ships and iron men: shipbuilding in Belfast, 1894–1912* (Belfast, 1989).   **56** For
information on the Welch photographs in Birmingham see http://www.birmingham.gov.uk

Wesley Historical Society, Belfast

1880–1950

Miscellaneous photographs relating to Methodists and Methodism in Ireland.
Wesley Historical Society Irish Branch, Aldersgate House, 9–11 University Road,
Belfast, BT 71NA.
Email: enquiry@uhf.org.uk

Westropp, Thomas J.[57]

1898–1921   32 photographic prints

Photographs taken by Thomas J. Westropp depicting Dublin streets and ruins in the
aftermath of the 1916 Rebellion and *c*.1,300 images of antiquities in 14 Irish
counties, though they mainly relate to Co. Clare.
National Photographic Archive, Meeting House Square, Temple Bar, Dublin 2.
Tel.: 01 6030371. Email: photoarchive@nli.ie More of his photographs are in The
National Museum of Ireland. An album of Westropp's photographs entitled 'Views
in County Clare 1898' is in Clare County Library, Mill Road, Ennis, Co. Clare. Tel.:
065 6821616. Email: mailbox@clarelibrary.ie

Wiltshire, Elinor & Reggie

1951–71   *c*.322 photographic prints and *c*.1,000 film negatives

Excellent black and white photographs taken in various parts of Ireland, including
several of Patrick Kavanagh.[58]
National Photographic Archive, Meeting House Square, Temple Bar, Dublin 2.
Tel.: 01 6030371. Email: photoarchive@nli.ie

Wynne Collection

1867–1960   *c*. 8,000 glass negatives

Important collection for all aspects of life in Castlebar and surrounding areas of Co.
Mayo.[59]
National Photographic Archive, Meeting House Square, Temple Bar, Dublin 2.
Tel.: 01 6030371. Email: photoarchive@nli.ie
Approximately 2,000 copy prints are held in Castlebar Library, Pavilion Road,
Castlebar, Co. Mayo.
Tel.: 094 9047513. Email: ihamrock@mayococo.ie

---

57 Some of Westrop's images are also to be found in the Royal Society of Antiquaries of
Ireland at 63 Merrion Square, Dublin 2. Tel.: 01 6761749. Email: rsai@rsai.ie   **58** Orla
Fitzpatrick, *If ever you go to Dublin town: photographs of Elinor Wiltshire* (Dublin, 1999).   **59** Art
Byrne & Seán McMahon, *Faces of the west, 1875–1925* (Dublin, 1976).

CHAPTER 4

Reading photographs

The photographic image, like all other images, speaks its own universal language and consequently can be read anywhere. However, some people consider photography as another form of writing. Susan Sontag compared photography to 'a handy, fast form of note-taking.'[1] Joseph N. Niépce called photography heliography or sun writing and Fox Talbot referred to the camera as a 'pencil of nature.' So in many senses one can regard the photographic image as a document which the historian needs to read and then translate into the vernacular language. Reading, evaluating and interpreting a photograph or other visual image is obviously a different process to reading, evaluating and interpreting a manuscript document.[2] Yet some of the same principles apply to both. The photographic image must given the same respect, time and attention one would give to any other primary source. When analysing photographs the following questions need to be asked:

1 *Is the photograph authentic?*
This is the first and perhaps the most important question one must ask of a photographic document. In the past it was claimed 'that the camera never lies' but now it is known that this is not true. With the digital and computer revolution of recent decades there is a new awareness that by using such techniques as airbrushing, smudging and super-imposing, almost anything can be done to alter an original photograph. Manipulation is, and always has been, possible at every stage of making a photograph.

The question of the authenticity of photographs is not a recent one. It was there from the beginning. In October 1840 the Frenchman Hippolyte Bayard produced a photograph named 'self-portrait as a drowned man' which purported to prove that he had drowned himself because the government, scientists and newspapers had failed to recognize his important role in the development of the camera.[3] It was an elaborate hoax. Bayard lived to the grand old age of 86, dying 35 years after he attempted to use a photograph to convey a message that was not true. In 1855 a German photographer, who had invented a technique for retouching calotype

---

1 Sontag, *On photography*, p. 6.   2 The Lewis Glucksman Gallery at University College Cork was aware that reading images is a different kind of reading and in September 2006 it launched an educational art pack called *The art of looking* for the younger visitors to their gallery. The photographer Dorothy Lange wrote that 'The camera is an instrument that teaches people how to see without a camera'. See Keith F. Davis, *The photographs of Dorothea Lange* (Kansas, 1995), p. 1. Dorothea Lange took photographs in Ireland in the 1950s. 3 Batchen, *Burning with desire*, pp 158–73; Frizot, *The new history of photography*, p. 30.

negatives, astounded crowds at the Exposition Universelle held in Paris with his two versions of the one portrait, one retouched, the other not.[4] Later Victorian photographers would develop a technique whereby two or more negatives could be imposed and processed on a single sheet of paper, producing a composite image.

The relationship between photography and painting was from the beginning of photography an uneasy one and the lines between them often blurred. One of the strengths of photography was that it was thought to be more authentic, more true to life than painting. Edward McParland, in his article 'Malton's views of Dublin: too good to be true?' looks critically at James Malton's aquatints and watercolours of Dublin city in the 1790s and suggests that they are idealized views of the city and less reliable than photographs might be because the perspectives were not produced on the spot but later in a London studio.[5] So too one could argue that some of the streetscape photographs of Dublin and of towns throughout Ireland, which were taken one hundred years later for the Lawrence photographic studio, were also idealized images which, like Malton's creations, needed to be approached with caution. Sometimes the painting can be more authentic and a more truthful representation than the photograph.

Leland Duncan's photograph of Mrs Mary Ward in Co. Leitrim in August 1892 is very similar to one taken by William A. Green in Inishowen in Co. Donegal about ten years later.[6] Both photographs depict a woman sitting outside her house beside a spinning wheel. These photographs seem to suggest that women did their spinning outdoors while the reality was that the photographers had the women and the spinning wheels positioned outdoors so that they would have sufficient light to take the picture. James Brenan's painting 'Interior, with woman spinning – study from nature, south of Ireland', which he painted *c*.1876, is therefore a more truthful representation in that it shows a woman spinning indoors as was the normal practice.[7] By 1933, availing of advances in cameras and flash-bulbs, Fr Frank Browne was able to take an excellent photograph of spinning indoors in Cloone, Co. Leitrim.[8] In 1952 George Pickow photographed Mrs Bartley Hernon working at her spinning wheel inside her house on Galway's Inishmore Island.[9] Tom Hussey's photograph of indoor spinning in the 1970s is more recent than most.[10] These twentieth-century photographs of indoor spinning therefore help to correct the misleading impression given by some of the outdoor photographs from the previous century.

4 Sontag, *On photography*, p. 86.   **5** Brian F. Kennedy & Raymond Gillespie (eds), *Ireland: art into history* (Dublin, 1994), pp 15–25.   **6** For Duncan's photograph see Kelly, *The face of time*, p. 56. For Green's photograph see the Ulster Folk and Transport Museum, WAG 1182. **7** Peter Murray (ed.), *Whipping the herring: survival and celebration in nineteenth-century Irish art* (Cork, 2006), pp 170–1. Note also the other depictions of indoor spinning in the paintings on pp 163, 167.   **8** O'Donnell, *Fr Browne's Ireland: remarkable images of people and places*, p. 105.   **9** The Ritchie-Pickow photographic collection is in the Hardiman Library, NUI Galway.   **10** Tom Hussey, *A bar of light* (Sligo, 2007), p. 43.

4.1 Photograph from the Lawrence collection of the eviction of John Flanagan in Co. Clare in July 1888 (LROY 1776) (courtesy of National Photographic Archive)

If we take a closer look at one of the Lawrence photographs of the eviction of John Flanagan off the Vandeleur estate in Co. Clare in July 1888 we will be able to further tease out the issue of a photograph's authenticity (see fig. 4.1). This photograph is obviously a posed, after-the-event photograph where all seems calm, orderly and peaceful. By contrast Henry Jones Thaddeus's painting 'An Irish eviction, County Galway, 1889' captures much more of the physicality and violence, the confusion and chaos that were an integral part of most evictions.[11]

In judging the authenticity of a photograph one needs to be mindful that the photographer takes an active role in creating the image. There usually is something of the stage-manager about the photographer. So some questions need to be asked – what in the photograph is moveable and what is not? In the moveable category what objects or people were deliberately placed by the photographer? Did any or all of the people in the photograph dress up for the occasion?

Photographs by press photographers and photojournalists can be very useful to historians – though they too need to treated with caution. Michael Langford explains that 'Occasionally photographers miss shots and ask the participants to repeat an event … taken to extremes it can lead to posed and totally manufactured

11 Murray (ed.), *Whipping the herring*, pp 136–7.

news situations.'[12] In addition, the photographer may inadvertently be responsible for manipulating the image. The very presence of a photographer may create an artificial situation as people often respond to the presence of the camera and duly perform for it.

In recent decades, with the arrival of digital cameras and personal computers, photographs can now be manipulated more radically and more easily than ever before. This has created a crisis in photography and raises the question 'can any photograph be believed?' Estelle Jussim was aware of this difficulty as early as April 1986. She wrote in the *Boston Review* of that month:

> Small wonder that photography finds itself in a state of crisis … No longer trusted for its presumed objectivity and transparency, no longer the reliable guide to visual 'truth' documentary photography has had its authority devastated by technologies …[13]

Digitization has revolutionized photography and created so great a crisis that some commentators are talking and writing about the 'death' of photography.[14]

> In fact, the new malleability of the image may eventually lead to a profound undermining of photography's status as an inherently truthful pictorial form … If even a minimal confidence in photography does not survive, it is questionable whether many pictures will have meaning anymore, not only as symbols, but as evidence.[15]

The historian needs to be more critical and more wary when using photographs as primary sources taken in the digital age. All photographs, however, from 1839 onwards, must be analysed critically and thoroughly for authenticity. Given the fact that distortion and manipulation were possible in every era of the camera and at every stage of the process of photographing, one is left wondering if photographs are of any use to historians as primary sources of information. The answer is a very definite 'yes'. Many photographs are completely authentic and even those that have been manipulated may contain some truth. The very fact that they have been manipulated is important in itself and may be of use to the researcher. The historian Arthur Marwick's advice applies to photographs as well as to other primary sources: He wrote 'In analysing primary sources, historians must be critical … [they must] always be sceptical, never cynical'.[16] Donovan Wylie, who was born in Belfast in 1971 and who has become one of Ireland's best present-day photographers, sees some positives in the digital camera and a bright future for photography. He wrote:

12 Michael Langford, *The complete encyclopaedia of photography* (London, 1982), p. 326. 13 Reprinted in Jussim, *The eternal moment*, p. 5.   14 For example see Batchen, *Burning with desire*, pp 206–8. Others are much more positive about the impact of the digital revolution on photography. See Jonathan Lipkin, *Photography reborn: image making in the digital era* (New York, 2005).   15 Fred Ritchin, 'Photojournalism in the age of computers' in Carol Squiers (ed.), *The critical image, essays in contemporary photography* (Seattle, 1990), pp 28, 37.   16 Arthur

Digital photography has cleared away a misconception that should have been cleared away at the very beginning of photography – the camera doesn't lie. Actually, the camera doesn't lie, photographers do. But photographers can also tell the truth, and that's what we should be concentrating on.[17]

2 *Where was the photograph taken?*

The more that is known about the provenance of a photograph the better one is able to decide on its authenticity. Sometimes it is very obvious where a photograph was taken because there is an easily recognizable landscape, streetscape, historic ruins or other building either in the foreground or background of the image. Other times we may recognize one or more people in the photograph but not the location, which may lessen its value as a primary source. Anna Godley, an amateur photographer and cousin of the Godley family who lived on the Kilbracken estate in Co. Leitrim, along with many other landed gentry photographers of the late nineteenth century, took photographs not just in Ireland, but also while holidaying in Italy or in other European countries. The photographs taken abroad, while still of interest to the local historian, will usually yield less useful information than those taken at home. However, these images may be the only documentary proof that the photographer and the people depicted in them did, in fact, travel abroad. Photographer tended to travel, or to put it another way, travellers tended to take photographs. The local historian must recognise this fact and search widely at home and abroad for photographs created by travelling photographers.

Once a photograph is captured by the camera and removed from the location it was taken in, it becomes a displaced document. Dorothea Lange, who took excellent photographs in Ireland in the 1950s, knew the importance of the photographer having a sense of place. She wrote 'whatever I photograph I try to picture it as parts of its surroundings, as having roots'.[18] The researcher must, as far as possible, restore the photograph to its birth-place, to its roots.

3 *Who took the photograph?*

The more information one can get on the creator of the document, the photographer, the more useful the photograph is likely to be to the history researcher. Photographers do much more than push a button to capture an image. They have a vital and active role to play before, during and after the picture is taken. A photograph is not merely the result of an encounter between an event and a photographer: it is an event in itself and one which is influenced profoundly by the individual taking the photograph. In that sense we see the image of the past not so much through the dispassionate lens of a camera as through the subjective eyes of the photographer:

Marwick, *The nature of history* (London, 1970), p. 225. **17** Cited in Badger, *The genius of photography*, p. 233. **18** Davis, *The photographs of Dorothea Lange*, p. 11.

4.2 This photograph by Fr Frank Browne was taken in 1938. The buildings in the background, which still survive, enable us to locate it in Virginia, Co. Cavan[19] (courtesy of Irish Picture Library)

19 O'Donnell, *Fr Browne's Ireland: remarkable images of people and places*, p. 33.

> The photographer [in the early years of photography] was thought to be an acute but non-interfering observer – a scribe, not a poet. But as people quickly discovered that no two people take the same picture of the same thing, the supposition that cameras furnish an impersonal, objective image yielded to the fact that photographs are evidence not only of what's there but of what an individual sees, not just a record but an evaluation of the world.[20]

Every photographer brings his or her own bias and prejudice, values and life experience to his or her camera work.[21] Ansel Adams (1902–84), a photographer best known for his black-and-white photographs of rural California, insists that we do not 'take' photographs, rather we 'make' them, and that a photograph is a concept and not an accident.[22] One cannot study a photograph in isolation from the individual who generated it. The photographer visualizes the image before the camera captures it. By choosing one image and omitting another, the photographer is thereby selecting and interpreting. The French film critic André Bazin played down the significance of the photographer's role in creating a photograph. He wrote:

> The personality of the photographer enters into the proceedings only in his selection of the object to be photographed and by way of the purpose he has in mind. Although the final result may reflect something of his personality, this does not play the same role as is played by that of the painter. All the arts are based on the presence of man, only photography derives an advantage from his absence.[23]

Few would agree with that viewpoint now. A photograph is not just a record of an event, it is also an expression of the photographer's own life. To understand a photograph, one needs to know about that life.

4 When was the photograph taken?
One of the tasks of the historian when working with photographs is to attempt to date them as accurately as possible. This important task may prove very difficult and challenging. Some photographers were very methodical and arranged their images into captioned albums, giving either a general date for the album or even particular dates for individual photographs. Others kept a notebook or diary which supplied dates and miscellaneous information relating to the photographs. If the photograph is an original positive print there is a slight chance that the date or other information might be written on it, either front or back.[24] Some studio photographs

20 Sontag, *On photography*, p. 88.   **21** Estelle Jussim states that we receive information from photographs 'through the cracked mirror of prejudice'. See Jussim, *The eternal moment*, p. 154.   **22** Cited in Sontag, *On photography*, pp 117, 123.   **23** André Bazin, 'The ontology of the photographic image' in Trachtenberg (ed.), *Classic essays on photography*, p. 241. **24** See the photograph by Lady Augusta Crofton Dillon at Clonbrock House (Fig. 2.2 above). It has the date it was taken 'Feb 20 / 64' handwritten on the bottom right of the image.

will have the studio stamp on the back of the image, and since the nature of this stamp changed over time, it too could help to date the photograph. However, more often than not, the researcher will have to work with a single photograph or a collection of photographs, positives or negatives, which bear no date at all. This poses a challenge to the researcher and yet every effort must be made to date the photograph as precisely as possible.

One approach to dating a photograph is to look at the physical properties of the artefact itself and try to discern the process that was used to produce it since different processes were used in different eras. Victorian positive images will, in most instances, be on metal, glass or paper.[25] If they are on metal they could be Daguerreotype or tintype. Tintype images, which are fixed on a black lacquered sheet of iron, can be quickly identified by using a small magnet. However, this may not be of much help in dating the photograph because tintype photography, which was invented in 1856 and was much used until 1870, continued in limited use until the 1960s. The Daguerreotype is a negative and has to be turned at a certain angle to the light for the image to appear. Daguerreotype images can safely be dated to the period 1840–60. Ambrotypes usually date from the period 1852–75. Glass plate negatives were used throughout the Victorian period and so are not much help in dating the image. Being able to distinguish if the glass plate image was fixed by the wet collodion process or by the dry plate method helps since the former was probably pre–1875 and the latter after that date.

If the positive image is paper-based then it should be possible to establish if it is an albumen coated, carbon or platinum print. The albumen coated prints were less widely used after 1880. The carbon printing method was started in 1864 and was used quite a lot in the period 1880 to 1930. The platinum prints began in 1874 and were used until World War I. The size of the print, the thickness of the glass plate and other physical properties are also used for dating nineteenth-century photographs.[26] All of this is an imprecise method of dating photographs and expert advice may be required to discern what type of photographic image it is and what period it may be attributed to. Besides, there was usually an over-lap between one method of photography and another, with the older method surviving in use sometimes for years, even decades, after a newer method had been developed.

A simpler method of dating old photographs is to study the dress-style and hair-style of the people featured in them. Noting women's dress-style may be

25 In the period 1850 to 1900 much experimentation took place and positive images were also developed on fabric, china, black leather, synthetic ivory and even wood and stone. **26** The Ulster Folk and Transport Museum has published a leaflet called 'The Victorian image, a brief guide to identifying and dating 19th-century photographs' which researchers may find useful. See also John Duggan, 'The origins of photography and its evolution in Ireland' a four-part series in *Irish roots*, no. 33, i (2000), pp 14–16, no. 34, ii (2000), pp 14–16, no. 35, iii (2000), pp 14–16, no. 36, iv (2000), pp 14–15. These short articles are accompanied by a list of 'nineteenth-century Irish photographers [listed] by name, location and approximate decade when active' which researchers may find useful in attempting to date nineteenth-century photographs.

particularly helpful, since their styles tended to change more often than men's. This requires some knowledge of the history of clothes, but the more knowledge one has of this, the more accurately one can date the photograph. It must be noted that dress-styles varied from place to place, from one age group to another and from one social class to another. Besides, there was always an over-lap in fashion too, with the older style lingering on for a time even when a new style was in vogue.[27]

Portrait photography changed from one era to another and studio photographs can be dated fairly accurately by noting the background, the pose and the angle the photographer chose and the distance the sitter was from the camera. In early Victorian portraits the subject tended to be farther away from the camera, giving a full-length image. As the Victorian period progressed, the distance between camera and subject lessened and by the 1890s most portraits were just head and shoulders or even head and neck shots. Robert Pols, in his book *Family photographs, 1860–1945*[28], details how the use of art work, curtains, head and back supports, furniture and other studio paraphernalia changed during this period and how one could date portraits, with some accuracy, by studying these changes.

Examining the background may also help to date outdoor photographs such as streetscapes or landscapes. William Henry Fox Talbot's famous photograph of the construction of Nelson's column in Trafalgar Square can be dated to the first week of April 1844 by the theatre bills posted on the hoardings.[29] The stereo photograph of Dublin's O'Connell bridge and of the Daniel O'Connell monument can be safely dated between the unveiling of the monument on 15 August 1882 and the adding of the Winged Victories the following year.[30] See fig. 4.3. Elinor Wiltshire photographed the truncated remains of Nelson's pillar in Dublin on 8 March 1966, the morning after it was bombed. Since the remainder of the pillar was later removed by army engineers, her photograph can be dated easily and accurately.[31] However, many photographs contain useful and much less obvious background details that may help date them. It could be the roofing material on a house, the model of a bicycle or car – with or without its number plate showing – the owner's name over a shop awning or the type of items displayed in the window. Such clues, taken in conjunction with other primary sources of information, can help one date a photograph with some assurance.

27 For information on the history of clothes and fashion in Ireland see Mairéad Dunleavy, *Dress in Ireland* (Cork, 1999); Linda Ballard, *Forgetting frolic: marriage traditions in Ireland* (Belfast, 1998); Lillias Mitchell, *Irish spinning, dyeing and weaving* (Dundalk, 1978); Anne O'Dowd, *Common clothes & clothing, 1860–1930* (Dublin, 1990). The National Museum of Ireland also produced a catalogue called *The way we wore: 250 years of Irish clothing and jewellery* in 2004. My thanks to Deirdre O'Connell for her help on the history of Irish fashion. **28** Robert Pols, *Family photographs, 1860–1945* (London, 2002), pp 56–65. This book, which was published as a genealogy guide by the Public Records Office in Kew, has a good section on methods of dating photographs. See also Audrey Linkman, *The expert guide to dating Victorian family photographs* (Manchester, 2000); James M. Reilly, *Care and identification of 19th-century photographic prints* (Rochester, NY, 1986). **29** Badger, *The genius of photography*, p. 18. **30** See the National Library of Ireland's production *Ireland 1860–80 from stereo photographs* (Dublin, 1981), no. 25. **31** Fitzpatrick, *If ever you go to Dublin town*, p. 73.

4.3 This Lawrence collection photograph of the O'Connell Bridge and monument can be dated to late 1882 or early 1883 by the base of the O'Connell statue (courtesy of National Photographic Archive)

It is always advisable for historians to study photographs alongside other contemporaneous primary source documents and not in isolation from them. Other primary sources can help to date photographs. For example, if the name of one or more people in the photograph is known, then it may be possible to glean details of their date of birth, marriage or death from church or civil records. If this information is known it should in turn be possible to judge with some accuracy their age at the time when the photograph was taken and in this way to date the photograph itself. This method of dating a photograph is not, however, without problems. Judging a person's age, especially from a photograph, is an imprecise science. It is difficult to gauge a person's age in one's own era. It is more difficult to do so with people from other eras. People tended to age more rapidly in the nineteenth century than they did in the twentieth century and people who lived their lives in impoverished conditions aged more quickly than those who did not.

BALLINAMORE AGRICULTURAL SHOW, SEPTEMBER 3, 1910.

4.4 Postcard image of Ballinamore, Co. Leitrim Agricultural show on 3 September 1910.

Picture postcards can be dated in the same way as other photographs and also by means peculiar to it. If the postcard was mailed, it may have a stamp mark or even a date written by the sender. Some postcards, such as the one of the Agricultural Show in Ballinamore, Co. Leitrim on 3 September 1910, have the date on which the picture was taken printed beneath the image.[32] See fig. 4.4. Picture postcards generally date from 1890 onwards. Before that it was more common to have a lithographic image over which the message was written. Postcards which have the reverse side divided in two – half for the address and half for the sender's message – date from 1902 or later. Previous to that all of the reverse side was taken up with the address. Colour picture postcards and colour photographs were rare before World War I. Many of the earlier coloured photographs were hand-painted and it is important to be able to distinguish between the two when trying to date a photograph. If the original photograph is available, close scrutiny with a magnifying glass may reveal the layer of added paint in hand-painted pictures.

A photograph can still be a good primary source for historians even if it is not possible to date it accurately. However, the more precisely one can date it, the more useful it will be as a reliable source of information. For example, we know from Leland L. Duncan's diary that he took several group photographs in the Kiltubrid area of Co. Leitrim on 15 August 1892. The fact that these photographs were taken on the afternoon of the Feast of the Assumption, after the families had returned from Mass, explains why they were so much better dressed that those in the other photographs Duncan took in the same area before and after that date.

32 I am indebted to P.J. Dunne who gave this postcard to me.

5 How was the photograph taken?
It may not be always possible to establish the type of camera or process the photographer used when taking the photograph but it will help the researcher's assessment
of it if this can be done. Understanding the way the photographic document was
produced helps the researcher to understand the document itself. A sense of the
technical history of photography will enrich any analysis of photographs.

For example, if the photograph was an outdoor, pre-1870 one which was taken
using the wet collodion process, the researcher needs to understand that the
photographer had to haul the large box camera and tripod, a variety of chemicals,
a supply of water and a portable tent to act as a dark room so that the photograph
could not only be taken but also developed on location before the plate had dried.
The amount of equipment, the long exposure time needed, together with the
complicated and difficult process involved in making a photograph, limited
considerably the number and type of photographs that could be taken. As a result
photographers seldom strayed far from the beaten path with their bulky and fragile
equipment. They tended to take their images near public roads or railway lines[33]
and they often avoided taking shots of children or animals because they were likely
to move during the long exposure time required. For Victorian photographers,
especially the first generation of photographers, it was easier to take a photograph
of the built environment, antiquities, landscape or other inanimate objects. The
researcher who knows the difficulties facing the photographers using this method
will better understand why they chose some images and not others and why people
appear so stiff and staid in them.[34]

The photographer who used a portable Kodak camera in the 1890s or a
miniature-sized digital camera in the 1990s faced virtually none of the problems
the early photographers faced. As cameras improved technically, the number of
photographers and the range of their images expanded greatly. Researchers,
therefore, need to be able to put themselves in the photographer's shoes and try to
understand the technical and other difficulties he or she faced.

6 Why was the photograph taken?
If we know what motivated the photographer to take a particular photograph then
we will be better able to understand, analyse and evaluate that image. A photograph
is a snapshot, a slice of space and time, which for some reason the photographer
decided to create. For example, some of William Despard Hemphill's photographs
are still life pictures which obviously required much preparation and great attention

33 Knowing how photographers travelled and how they transported their cameras and other
equipment can help the researcher understand their selection of photographs. It is advisable
to study the photographs alongside a contemporary map showing road, rail and water
systems of transport.   **34** The long exposure time needed meant that the Victorian
photographer's last words to the people he was photographing was not 'say cheese' or 'smile'
but the strict order 'Don't move!'

4.5 The reason this Congested Districts Board photograph was taken in Cappagh, Co. Galway was to show how bad the conditions were there (courtesy of National Photographic Archive)

to detail. His motivation for taking aesthetically pleasing photographs was to produce works of art which he hoped would win a prize when he showed them at photographic exhibitions in Dublin, London or Paris.

Robert J. Welch was the main photographer employed by the Congested Districts Board to take photographs along the west coast of Ireland in the period 1895–1914. The reason these photographs were taken was to show some of the impoverished conditions people were living and working in and also to show how the Congested Districts Board was doing something to improve their conditions. By understanding this dual motivation the researcher will be better able to evaluate and interpret the photographs. Many of the images taken by the Lawrence, Eason and Valentine photographers, especially from 1890 onwards when postcards were becoming popular, were produced for purely commercial purposes. This explains why towns, historic sites, scenic views and tourist areas were photographed repeatedly while other areas, particularly sparsely populated areas, were ignored. Photographs which were taken in order to be sold, either as portraits or postcards, tended to idealize.

4.6 This Congested Districts Board's photograph, dated *c.*1900, suggests prosperity and displays the new house it built for Mrs Bridget Kelly from Lisavalley, Co. Galway (courtesy of National Photographic Archive)

One could argue that studio photographers had a more passive role than other photographers and consequently that knowing their motivation for taking photographs is less instructive. They took photographs on request and to make money from doing so. However, the historian must also be mindful of the motivation of the person who is having his or her photograph taken. Before 1839 only the wealthy could have their portraits painted. With the development of the camera and photographic studios many more of the less well-off could aspire to have their portraits taken quickly and relatively cheaply. A studio photograph of an individual, married couple or even whole family was a statement, not just that they could afford to have their photograph taken, but more importantly it was a statement to the wider society, that the family was relatively rich and successful.

7 What information is contained in the photograph?
There is a risk that photographs, like other visual images, will not be afforded the time or attention they deserve in order to extract all the information or evidence contained in them. Photographs can give a false impression that they can be read easily and quickly and so very often they just get a cursory glance from the researcher before they are left aside. Frequently the reader's eye will be drawn to

4.7 This postcard image of the Fair Green in Navan, Co. Meath *c.*1960 is from the Cardall collection. By zooming in on the back of the commercial van on the right hand side of the image we see that it reads: 'M. Murtagh & Sons/Wholesale/Grocer, Confectioner & Tobacconist/47 North Circular Rd/ Phone 70185' (courtesy of National Photographic Archive)

one section of the image – usually the centre portion – with the result that other sections may be neglected completely. A photograph must be studied systematically and forensically by the historian in order to make the best use of it as a primary source.

One way to do this is to grid the image into rectangular sections, much like an archaeologist would grid an archaeological site. Then, by studying each grid systematically and thoroughly, the researcher will be able to draw up an inventory of all the evidence contained in the photograph. It helps if the photographic image can be scanned onto a computer. By zooming in on a particular grid one enlarges it considerably and so it becomes possible to pick out detail not readily identifiable when one studies the image in its original size. Only when a particular grid is scanned thoroughly does one move onto the next grid. When analysed in a methodical way the researcher will be surprised by the amount of information the photograph yields. Some of the information gleaned in this way may suggest much staging by the photographer. This is important information in itself and it does not mean that the researcher cannot use that information or indeed any other evidence extracted from the photograph.

The photograph featured in figure 4.8 is divided into grids in order to study it systematically. Grid 1A is enlarged and studied in detail before moving on to 1B. This process is continued until finally grid 3L is reached. Grid 1A yields a surprise. Standing precariously on the window ledge is one of the domestic staff who,

4.8 The pupils and teaching staff of St Patrick's College, Cavan, pictured outside the college in 1927

unknown to the people in the main group, climbed out the refectory window to get a look at the proceedings. Thus he represents staff members otherwise excluded from the photograph. The row 3A to 3L, at first glance would appear to offer little information, but when enlarged and studied closely, this row yields considerable evidence about the type of boots, shoes, socks and trousers worn by the students in 1927.

The photograph in figure 4.9 is also divided into grids in order to extract information from it in a systematic way. Not every grid will yield useful information. The first four grids (1A to 1D) show the top sections of two rather gaunt trees which may not be of much interest to historians unless they are researching the scarcity and poor quality of trees in Leitrim at this time.[35] Grid 3B shows Mikey Lynch holding his hat in his right hand. This raises some questions: did he take off his hat in deference to the English gentleman taking his photograph or did the photographer ask him to do so? Grid 3C yields the more telling information that the subject's left hand is clenched tightly into a fist – most likely because he is nervous at seeing a camera and having his photograph taken for the first time. Duncan took several other photographs of Mikey Lynch between August 1889 and August 1894 and he seems much more at ease in the later photographs.[36]

Arthur Marwick, very usefully, divides information extracted from primary

---

35 Henry Doran, in his 1895 report to the Congested Districts Board on the parish of Kiltubrid (where this photograph was taken) deplored the lack of trees in the area and recommended that people be helped by 'providing them with suitable trees at a low price, and to exercise skilled supervision over their planting to ensure their growth.' Morrissey (ed.), *On the verge of want*, p. 75. Duncan took over 150 photographs in the area between 1889 and 1894 and these photographs, taken together, provide important documentary evidence on the lack of trees in the area at this time.   **36** See Kelly, *The face of time*, pp 40, 41, 57, 65; idem, *Kiltubrid: County Leitrim*, pp 51–3.   **37** Marwick, *The nature of history*, p. 218.

A   B   C   D

4.9 Mikey Lynch, at Annadale, Co. Leitrim. This photograph was taken by Leland L. Duncan in August 1889 (courtesy of Elizabeth Mans)

sources into 'witting' and 'unwitting testimony.'[37] The witting testimony is what the creator of the document, in this instance the photographer, intended to convey in the first place. The unwitting testimony is that which the document conveys without its creator either intending it or being aware of it at all. This is one of the great strengths of the camera. It, unlike the artist painting, captures unintended detail that may be invaluable to the researcher. This unwitting testimony is very often the evidence that is most useful to the historian. The Danish film historian, Karsten Fledelius, made a similar point about the medium of film:

> Often the most interesting evidence is the 'unwitting testimony' of the cinematographic recordings, all those incidental aspects of reality which have just 'slipped' into the camera without consciously being recorded by the cameraman. The 'evidence by accident' may be extremely valuable to the historian.[38]

This 'evidence by accident' is present in many photographs. It is evidence that we access, not through the subjective eye of the photographer, but rather through the neutral lens of the camera. It is often this minute detail and accidental information that makes researching photographic documents worthwhile.

38 Karsten Fledelius, 'Film and history – an introduction to the theme' in Comité International des Sciences Historiques, *XVI Congrés International des Sciences Historiques: Rapports*, 1, p. 186, quoted in Marwick, *The nature of history*, p. 218.

CHAPTER 5

Using photographic evidence

A photograph is a mere frame, a fragment.[1] It may, however, be a very important fragment. It is also a displaced document which has been removed from its context. A photograph can be usefully understood as a single grid of a large archaeological site or even as an item of archaeological significance which has been removed from its context. The task of the historian then, when using that photograph for research, is not just to see what information is contained in the image but also to attempt to restore it to its original context. This can be a painstaking and time-consuming process. It is, however, a necessary one. The context is not just about time and place. It is also about the social, cultural, political, religious and intellectual world in which the image was created. It is about understanding what influenced the photographer and what kind of images other photographers and artists were making at that time. It is also about understanding the impact these images had at their time. Once the photograph has been analysed and placed in context, it may well prove to be a document of considerable historical importance.

Laura Jones, in an article entitled 'Photography and ethnological research', warns of 'the need for caution in drawing conclusions on the basis of photographic evidence alone.'[2] This is not to denigrate photographic evidence; rather it is good advice, not just about photographic documents, but about all other primary sources. The best practice for historians is to gather the maximum number and greatest variety of primary sources available, analyse and interpret them and place them all alongside one another so that they may all enter dialogue with one another. The more sources one has, the more varied those sources are and the more thoroughly they are analysed, the more reliable one's conclusions will be. A single documentary source, photographic or otherwise, is a shaky foundation to build on. So whenever possible photographic evidence ought to be used alongside evidence gleaned from several other sources.

> Perhaps a single photograph or one group of photographs is an enigmatic and uncertain witness of history … Photographs are certainly not 'pure' documentary records and usually need supplementary documentation, such as words, before they can function as prime witnesses.[3]

1 Susan Sontag makes this point several times in her writing. See *On photography*, p. 71. In her most recent book, *At the same time* (New York, 2007), a book of her essays and speeches published three years after her death, she wrote that 'A photograph is a fragment – a glimpse.' (p. 126)   **2** Laura Jones, 'Photography and ethnological research' in *Ulster Folklife*, 26 (1980), p. 65.   **3** Badger, *The genius of photography*, p. 92.

A single photograph, no matter how good it is, has limited value for the historian and one must be careful about drawing conclusions from it. However, when there is a critical mass of photographs from a particular place and time, then the photographic evidence, in itself, can be quite compelling. For example, Leland L. Duncan took approximately 150 photographs of people in the parish of Kiltubrid, Co. Leitrim, between the years 1889 and 1894. He photographed males and females of different age groups in many different situations and on different days of the week in their working clothes and in their Sunday clothes. This body of photographic evidence built up by Duncan allows us to begin drawing certain conclusions about the way people dressed in this place and time. Photographs, paintings and sketches capture the dress-style of a place and period in a way that the written word cannot do.

William McKinney took excellent photographs in Co. Antrim at the end of the nineteenth and the beginning of the twentieth century. He used his camera to document life in the rural community of Carnmoney where he lived. One of his photographs, which was taken in 1910, shows John Condy dressed formally in a three-piece suit, cravat, bowler hat and watch chain, standing against the background of a substantial house and a rose-bush in full bloom.[4] The photograph is more about John Condy's new bicycle, which he displays in the photograph, than it is about the man himself or the house in the background. But while we can safely conclude that in the spring or early summer of 1910 this particular man had a new bicycle, we cannot draw any conclusions about the prevalence of bicycles, new or otherwise, in Carnmoney at this time. We need to ask the question 'did William McKinney photograph this man and his bicycle because having a bicycle was commonplace or because it was exceptional at this time?' The house in the background, the clothes that he was wearing and the fact that he was a National School teacher, would suggest that he was a man of means, unlike some others in the community, and so could afford to buy the new bicycle.[5] Chances are that having a new bicycle was the exception rather than the rule in Carnmoney at this time, though the photographic evidence does not allow us to draw this conclusion. Researchers must be careful not to generalize from the particular or extrapolate any conclusions from photographic evidence that are not warranted.

The early photographers liked to take photographs of the built environment – streetscapes, houses and historic ruins – because the definition of the finished image was usually good and because there was no danger of the solid buildings moving during the long exposure time.[6] People, whenever possible, prepared themselves for

---

4 Walker, *Sentry Hill: an Ulster farm and family*, p. 65. 5 Another of McKinney's photographs, taken in 1892 shows Miss G. Strahan sitting on a bicycle. 6 There is a famous streetscape photograph in the Stadtmuseum in Munich which was taken by Daguerre in Paris in 1839. It is a view of the Boulevard du Temple which shows the buildings in great detail but does not show any of the traffic or the people walking on the busy street – except a shoe-shine boy and the man who was getting his shoes polished who were stationary long enough for their picture to be captured by the camera. See Frizot, *The new history of photography*, p. 28.

5.1 Fr Frank Browne's photograph of the grand staircase at Rockingham House, Co. Roscommon in 1948. The house was destroyed by fire in 1957 (courtesy of Irish Picture Library).

photographs. This is not an issue with the built environment. In that sense it is easier to read a photograph of a building than it is to read one with people or other moveable objects in it. From the beginning the camera took kindly to buildings. It could record them accurately and in great detail. And very often photographs provide the best documentary evidence on the built environment.[7] The 1901 Census gives important details about each dwelling house in the country. It tells what materials the walls and roofing are made of, the number of rooms in the house and the number of windows it has. The Ordnance Survey map may even show the position of the house. But the researcher will still not know what it looked like. The photograph, when available, will complete the picture.

Photographs of quite a few big houses in Ireland have survived. These are important records now since many of these houses have disappeared either because they were destroyed during the War of Independence or later or because they crumbled due to neglect and the ravages of time. For example, Fr Frank Browne's magnificent 1948 photographs of Rockingham House, at Lough Key, Co. Roscommon[8] are more important now because the house is completely demolished.

The pioneer photographer W.H.F. Talbot noted that the camera was especially suited for recording 'the injuries of time'.[9] He was referring in particular to what happens to buildings and monuments. It is one of the great strengths of the camera that it can record what a building looks like at a specific time and then contrast that with how it looks 25, 50 or 100 years later. Time and human beings conspire together to change the built environment and the camera is ideally suited to record these changes. Camillio José Vergara has documented urban decay throughout the United States since 1977 with his camera and pen. His book *American ruins*[10] is a beautiful and poignant production which demonstrates how effectively and even artistically the camera can document destruction of the built environment. Many others have used photographs to document changes in the built environment here in Ireland. Louise Jefferson's book *Dublin then and now: scenes from a revolutionary city*[11] is a good example. It shows full-page, black-and-white photographs of Dublin in the period 1916–23 on one page and recent full-colour photographs of the same view on the opposite page. It too demonstrates how the camera can capture this change better than any amount of words can.[12] The Lawrence photographic project collection, comprising approximately 1,000 colour photographs taken in 1990, gives more recent views of some of the views in the original Lawrence collection. These 1990 photographs were taken by a group of 77 photographers in the Federation of Local History Societies and the Federation for Ulster Local Studies.[13] The juxtaposing of two photographs of the same building or streetscape which were

7 Toby Barnard, *A guide to sources for the history of material culture in Ireland, 1500–2000* (Dublin, 2005).   **8** O'Donnell, *Fr Browne's Ireland: remarkable images of people and places*, p. 109. **9** Cited in Sontag, *On photography*, p. 69.   **10** Camillio José Vergara, *American ruins* (New York, 1999).   **11** Louise Jefferson, *Dublin then and now: scenes from a revolutionary city* (Belfast, 2006).   **12** Many provincial towns have produced their own versions. For example Carrick on Shannon & District Historical Society published *Carrick-on-Shannon past and present: a pictorial record* in 2002.   **13** Rouse, *Into the light*, p. 57.

taken years apart creates its own dialogue and tells its story, often without the need for words.

Not only can historians compare photographs of the same place taken in different eras – they can also compare and contrast photographs taken in the same era in different localities. Leland L. Duncan's photographs taken in Co. Leitrim in the years 1889–94 can usefully be compared with those of William F. McKinney who was trying to build up a photographic record of farming practices in Co. Antrim at the same time Duncan was doing so in Co. Leitrim. McKinney's photographs show agricultural practises in Co. Antrim which were centred on the horse and horse-drawn machines such as rollers, hay-rakes, rick-shifters, reaping machines, swing ploughs and horse carts. Duncan's photographs depict farming practices in Co. Leitrim which are not nearly so advanced as those in Antrim and which depended largely on the donkey and hand-held tools to get the work done. The farm-sheds in McKinney's photographs are large free-standing buildings, erected with steel and roofed with galvanized corrugated iron whereas those featured in Duncan's photographs are small stone-walled, thatched-roofed buildings which in most cases are attached to the dwelling houses. The fact that these men took so many photographs of the farming practises in two different locations in Ireland means that we can begin to build up a picture of the very different methods of farming in these areas from the photographic evidence alone. When the photographic evidence is used alongside other documentary evidence[14] from Antrim and Leitrim we are able to conclude that not only the quality of the land but also the farming practices in these two counties were worlds apart in the 1890s.[15]

DISCOVERING AND HANDLING OLD PHOTOGRAPHS

Photographers have been creating images for almost 170 years. The photographic collections listed above in chapter three will give some indication of the vast number of photographic documents available for research. Some collections relating to Ireland are in public libraries, museums or archives either in Ireland or abroad, and much good work has been done cataloguing these in recent years. Some however, have yet to be catalogued and so are more challenging for researchers. Many other collections and individual photographs are in private hands and may not yet be available to historians for research. Privately owned photographs such as the one shown in figure 5.2 can be invaluable source material for the local historian.[16]

14 A good source for farming methods in Antrim at this time are McKinney's own letters and diaries. Henry Doran's report to the Congested Districts Board in 1895 gives a good insight into farming methods in Leitrim at this time.   15 Kelly, *Kiltubrid, County Leitrim*, pp 27–9.   16 My thanks to the Gaffney family, Crosskeys, for allowing me to use this photograph.

5.2 This photograph was taken in Crosskeys, Co. Cavan, during the 1918 general election. The building is the RIC barracks which had been vacated some months earlier.

The local historian seems particularly well placed to discover photographic images and, with the help of others, to identify, catalogue, date, secure and preserve them. Preserving them is a critical task since some are unstable and deteriorating. These images survive in many forms. Some are the original positive image on paper which may be loose or in an album. Others are negatives on celluloid or plate glass negatives. The plate glass negatives may be either the collodion wet plate negative or the later gelatin dry plate type. Others may be on a metal or an alternative solid base and may still be in their original frame or case. The researcher needs to know that the frame, case or material on which the image is based or even the album in which it is placed may be at least as significant historically as the image itself.

Researchers need to be aware that photographic images, either positive or negative, are very fragile items. They are at their most vulnerable when they have been discovered and moved from where they were stored. They can be damaged by being handled improperly, by changes in exposure to light, in humidity and in room temperature. The image should be held by the edges so that the print surface will not be touched by hand. Gloves should be worn when handling either negatives or positives so that one's hands do not damage the chemically-generated image. All desk surfaces must be clean and if it is necessary to write on the back of a paper-based image, it should be done with the softest of pencils and the minimum of writing. No ball-point pens or ink-based pens should be used, nor should any food or drink be allowed near them.

Paper-based images should be stored one on top of the other rather than on their edge so as to avoid curling of the image. Glass plate negatives, on the other hand, should be stored on their edge with the longest side facing down since they are too heavy to stack one on top of another. No two photographs should have their image side facing each other. Glass plate negatives and original positive images are often best stored in separate, specially designed paper envelopes. Old photographic images should be disturbed as little as possible and handled with exceptional care.[17] If possible they should be reformatted in order to preserve them and to provide the researcher with a copy to work on without interfering with the original image. With new developments in digital technology, the reformatting process is now much easier than it was in the past.

Local historians must know the limitations of their knowledge and skills in dealing with old photographs. The handling, care and preservation of them should, as far as possible, be left to those with expertise in this area. By working with library and museum staff and by co-operating with conservators and conservationists who specialise in old photographic images, historians will avoid doing damage to photographs and also may learn much from these specialists about the date of the image, the method used to create it and other information which will be invaluable in their research.

17 For more information on good practice in handling and preserving photographs see Reilly, *Care and identification of 19th-century photographic prints*; Pols, *Family photographs, 1860–1945*, especially chapter seven 'Preserving and collecting old photographs', pp 131–40. The American Museum of Photography has a helpful website entitled 'Preserving & protecting photographs'. See http://www.photographymuseum.com/archival.html (8 Feb. 2008).

Conclusion

Historians have, in the past, shied away from using photographs and other visual images, as primary sources in their research. They tended to have a hierarchy of primary sources with written sources ranking top and visual images coming last or perhaps even not being considered at all. This neglect may have been due to the fact that some researchers who can analyse and extract information from a manuscript document with relative ease often struggle when it comes to analysing photographs and other visual sources. Many of the Victorian photographers used both camera and pen, writing letters or diaries contemporaneously with their camera work. Why then should historians value what these people created with the pen more than what they created with the camera?

Many historians use photographs at the publication stage of their work rather than at the research stage. They use them merely to embellish the written word, the already closed research. As a result the photographs which were used by historians often bore little relation to the accompanying text and errors were more likely to occur when captioning the photographs than in the main body of the text because the writer had paid less attention to this aspect of his or her publication. Little attempt was made to place the photographs in their original context.

> In Ireland historians still regard images as sideshow to the main task of interpreting written documents from the past … Images are rarely treated as evidence in themselves … Visual images can be a powerful tool for understanding the past and deserve to be treated not merely as illustrations or appendages to a text but as documents, to be read in conjunction with other contemporary material …[1]

This situation has improved in recent years. It is now generally accepted that the photographic image is a document, just as much as a government report, contemporary account or other written source is. Historians are now more likely to approach their research in a multi-faceted way using photographs, film, paintings, sketches, literature, maps, the built environment, landscape, oral history and archaeology as well as other written sources in their research. Increasingly photographs are being given the attention and respect that they deserve. They must, however, be there from the beginning of the research process and not inserted at the end, as an after-thought to prettify. Photographs have their limitations as primary sources, but when approached in a critical and thorough fashion and when taken in conjunction with other sources they have much to contribute to the research and writing of history.

[1] Kennedy & Gillespie (eds), *Ireland: art into history*, p. 7.

If we accept that a photograph is a document which may contain important information useful to the historian then these photographic documents must be evaluated, interpreted and analysed in a systematic and thorough way. The photographic image can lure the researcher into believing that it is an easily accessible primary source and that a cursory glance at it will suffice. Looking at a photograph can appear less challenging than trying to decipher an almost illegible manuscript which may need to be translated. Yet the historian must interrogate the photograph in the same way and with the same thoroughness he or she would approach any other primary source. Old photographs need to be approached with a certain caution. They can draw researchers in, disarm them and blur their judgement in a cloud of sentimentality.

> Photographs turn the past into an object of tender regard, scrambling moral distinctions and disarming historical judgments by the generalized pathos of looking at time past.[2]

Researching and reading photographic images can and should be an enjoyable experience, though the researchers must ensure that their critical faculty remains intact while doing so.

People have been creating photographic documents for almost 170 years. There is now a vast number of photographic documents waiting to be analysed and researched. These documents have much information useful to our understanding of the past and they will reward the historian who takes the time to read them.

---

2 Sontag, *On photography*, p. 71.

Select bibliography

Annan, Thomas, *Photographs of the old closes and streets of Glasgow, 1868–1877* (Glasgow, 1878).

Anonymous, *Carrick-on-Shannon past and present: a pictorial record* (Carrick-on-Shannon, 2002).

Anonymous, *Hugh Doran, photographer* (Dublin, 2007).

Anonymous, *Hindesight: photographs and postcards by John Hinde Ltd, 1935–1971* (Dublin, 1993).

Anonymous, *RTÉ off camera* (Dublin, 2004).

Anonymous, *The origins of British photography* (Paris, 1988).

Anonymous, *The way we wore: 250 years of Irish clothing & jewellery* (Dublin, 2004).

Badger, Gerry, *The genius of photography: how photography has changed our lives* (London, 2007).

Ballard, Linda, *Forgetting frolic: marriage traditions in Ireland* (Belfast, 1998).

Bardon, Jonathan, *Belfast: a century* (Belfast, 1999).

Barnard, Toby, *A guide to sources for the history of material culture in Ireland, 1500–2000* (Dublin, 2005)

Batchen, Geoffrey, *Burning with desire: the conception of photography* (Boston, 1997).

Beattie, Seán, *Donegal, Ireland in old photographs* (Gloucester, 2004).

Bell, Fergus Hanna, *Newry, Warrenpoint & Rostrevor: early photographs from the Lawrence collection, 1865–80* (Belfast, 1989).

Bell, Jonathan & Mervyn, Watson, *Farming in Ulster: historic photographs of Ulster farming and food* (Belfast, 2004).

Berger, John, *Ways of seeing* (London, 1972).

Bolton, Richard (ed.), *The contest of meaning: critical histories of photography* (Boston, 1992).

Breathnach, Caoilte & Anne, Korff, *Kinvara: a seaport town on Galway bay* (Galway, 1997).

Breathnach, Ciara, *The Congested Districts Board of Ireland, 1891–1923* (Dublin, 2003).

— (ed.), *Framing the west: images of rural Ireland, 1891–1920* (Dublin, 2007).

Buckland, Gail, *The magic image: the genius of photography from 1839 to the present day* (London, 1975).

— *Fox Talbot and the invention of photography* (Boston, 1980).

— & Cecil Beaton, *Reality recorded: early documentary photographs* (New York, 1974).

Burnett-Brown, A., M. Gray & R. Roberts (eds), *Specimens and marvels: William Henry Fox Talbot and the invention of photography* (Bradford, 2000).

Byrne, Art & Seán McMahon, *Faces of the west, 1875–1925* (Dublin, 1976).

Cadogan, T., *Cobh in old picture postcards* (Zaltbommel, 1995).

Cartier-Bresson, Henri, *The decisive moment: photographs by Henri Cartier-Bresson* (New York, 1952).

Casserley, H.C., *Irish railways in the heyday of steam* (Dublin, n.d.).

Chandler, Edward, *Photography in Dublin in the Victorian era* (Dublin, 1980).

— *Photography in Ireland, the nineteenth century* (Dublin, 2001).

— & Peter Walsh, *Through the brass lidded eye* (Dublin, 1989).

Coe, Brian, *The birth of photography: the formative years, 1800–1900* (London, 1976).

Coote, Jack, *The illustrated history of colour photography* (London, 1993).

Corcoran, Doreen, *A tour of East Antrim: historic photographs from the W.A. Green collection in the Ulster Folk and Transport Museum* (Belfast, 1990).

Corr, Ben, *From the mountains to the sea: photographs of the people of Mourne, 1955–75* (Belfast, 1989).

Coughlan, Stephen (ed.), *Picture that: a century of Cork memories* (Cork, 1986).

— (ed.), *Picture that again* (Cork, 1986).

Coulston, Bill, *Images of life* (Cavan, 2007).

Crosbie, Jane E., *A tour of north Down, 1895–1925* (Belfast, 1989).

Curtin, Seán, *Limerick: a stroll down memory lane* (6 vols, Limerick, 2002–6).

Davis, Keith F., *The photographs of Dorothea Lange* (Kansas, 1995).

Davis, William C., *The Civil War in photography* (London, 2002).

Davison, David, *Impressions of an Irish Countess* (Dublin, 1989).

Dodier, Virginia, *Lady Clementina Hawarden: studies of life, 1857–1864* (London, 1999).

Doyle, Bill, *The Aran Islands – another world* (Dublin, 1995).

—, *The magic and mystery of Ireland* (Dublin, 1998).

—, *The images of Dublin: a time remembered* (Dublin, 2001).

Doyle, Colman, *All changed: fifty years of photographing Ireland* (Dublin, 2004).

— and Liam Flynn, *Ireland 40 years of photo-journalism* (Dublin, 1994).

Dunleavy, Mairéad, *Dress in Ireland* (Cork, 1999).

Dunne, P.J., *County Cavan in old picture postcards with historical commentary* (Cavan, 2000).

Dwyer, K., *Ireland, our island home* (Cork, 1977).

Evans, E.E. & B.S. Turner, *Ireland's eye: the photographs of Robert Welch* (Belfast, 1996).

Evans, Eric J. & Richards, Jeffrey, *A social history of Britain in postcards, 1870–1930* (London, 1980).

Fay, William & G. Carswell, *The Fays of the Abbey Theatre: an autobiographical record* (London, 1935).

Fitzgibbon, Jimmy, *A time and a place, New Ross, 1890–1910: a photographic record of the time* (New Ross, 2007).

Fitzpatrick, Orla, *If ever you go to Dublin town* (Dublin, 1999).

Flanders, S., *The County Donegal railway: an Irish railway pictorial* (London, 1996).

Freedman, Jill, *A time that was: Irish moments* (London, 1987).

Frizot, Michael (ed.), *The new history of photography* (Paris, 1994).

Gernsheim, Helmut, *The origins of photography* (New York, 1982).

— , *The rise of photography 1850–1880: the age of collodion* (New York, 1988).

Gernsheim, Helmut & Alison, *A concise history of photography* (London & New York, 1965).

Griffin, Des, *A parcel from the past: Waterford as seldom seen before* (Waterford, 1994).

Hamilton, Roy, *100 years of Derry* (Belfast, 1999).

Harrison Therman, Dorothy, *Stories from Tory Island* (Dublin, 1989).

Healy, Dermot (ed.), *A bar of light: Tom Hussey* (Sligo, 2007).

Hemphill, William Despard, *The abbeys, castles and scenery of Clonmel* (Dublin, 1860).

Hickey, Kieran, *The light of other days, Irish life at the turn of the century in the photographs of Robert French* (London, 1973).

Hill, Myrtle & Vivienne Pollock, *Women of Ireland: image and experience c.1880–1920* (Belfast, 1993).

—, *Image and experience: photographs of Irishwomen c.1880–1920* (Belfast, 1993).

Hirsch, Robert, *Seizing the light: a history of photography* (New York, 2000).

Holland, Pat, *Tipperary images: the photographs of Dr William Despard Hemphill* (Cahir, 2003).

International Federation of Library Associations and Institutions, *Care, handling and storage of photographs* (Washington DC, 1992).

Jefferson, Louise, *Dublin then and now: scenes from a revolutionary city* (Belfast, 2006).

Jeffrey, Ian, *Photography: a concise history* (London, 1981).

Jordan, Thomas E., *An imaginative empiricist – Thomas Aiskew Larcom (1801–1879) and Victorian Ireland* (Dublin, 2002).

Jussim, Estelle, *The eternal moment: essays on the photographic image* (New Jersey, 1989).

Kearns, S., *1894–1994: The centenary of the picture postcard in Ireland* (Dublin, 1994).

Kelly, Liam, *The face of time* (Dublin, 1995).

—, *Kiltubrid, County Leitrim: snapshots of a rural parish in the 1890s* (Dublin, 2005).

Kemp, Martin (ed.), *Masterworks of photography from the University of St Andrew* (Edinburgh, 1996).

Kennedy, Brian P. & Raymond Gillespie (eds), *Ireland: art into history* (Dublin, 1994).

Kiely, B. *The aerofilms book of Ireland – from the air* (London, 1985).

Kissane, Noel, *The Irish face* (Dublin, 1986).

—, *Ex camera 1860–1960: photographs from the collections of the National Library of Ireland* (Dublin, 1990).

Langford, Michael, *The complete encyclopaedia of photography* (London, 1982).

Lenman, Robin (ed.), *The Oxford companion to the photograph* (Oxford, 2005).

Lincoln, Colm, *Dublin as a work of art* (Dublin, 1992).

Linkman, Audrey, *The expert guide to dating Victorian family photographs* (Manchester, 2000).

Lipkin, Jonathan, *Photography reborn: image making in the digital era* (New York, 2005).

Mackey, Brian, *Lisburn: the town and its people, 1873–1973* (Belfast, 2000).

MacWeeney, Alen, *Irish travellers, tinkers no more* (Henniker, NH, 2007).

— & Michael Conniff, *Irish walls* (New York, 1986).

— & Sue Allison, *Bloomsbury reflections* (New York, 1990).

Maguire, W.A., *Caught in time: the photographs of Alexander Hogg of Belfast* (Belfast, 1990).

—, *A century in focus: photographs and photography in the north of Ireland, 1839–1939* (Belfast, 2000).

Martin, Donald, *Killybegs then and now* (Dublin, 1998).

Marwick, Arthur, *The nature of history* (London, 1970).

McCaughan, Michael, *Steel ships and iron men: shipbuilding in Belfast, 1894–1912* (Belfast, 1989).

McCullough, Niall, *Dublin: an urban history* (Dublin, 2007).

McDonnell, Ian & Finbar McCauley (eds), *Criminal justice history: themes and controversies from pre-independence Ireland* (Dublin, 2002).

McParland, Edward & David Davison, *Public architecture in Ireland, 1680–1760* (Yale, 2001).

Meyer, Carol, *Becoming: the photographs of Clementina Viscountess Hawarden* (London, 1999).

Micks, William L., *An account of the constitution, administration and dissolution of the Congested Districts Board from 1889 to 1923* (Dublin, 1925).

Mitchell, Lillias, *Irish spinning, dyeing & weaving* (Dundalk, 1978).

Morrissey, James (ed.), *On the verge of want* (Dublin, 2001).

Murphy, David, *Irish regiments in the world wars* (Oxford, 2007).

Murphy, Niall, *A bloomsday postcard* (Dublin, 2004).

Murray, Peter (ed.), *Whipping the herring: survival and celebration in nineteenth-century Irish art* (Cork, 2006).

Newhall, Beaumont, *The history of photography from 1839 to the present* (New York, 1982).

Nolan, Matt, *Mullingar: just for the record* (Dublin, 1999).

Nyhan, Miriam, *Are you still below? The Ford marina plant, Cork, 1917–1984* (Cork, 2007)

O'Brien, Gearóid, *Athlone in old photographs* (Dublin, 2002).

O'Connell, Michael, *Shadows, an album of the Irish people, 1841–1914* (Dublin, 1985).

O'Donnell, E.E., *The annals of Dublin* (Dublin, 1987)

—, *Father Browne's Ireland: remarkable images of people and places* (Dublin, 1989).

—, *The genius of Father Browne* (Dublin, 1990).

—, *Forest images* (Dublin, 1992).

—, *Father Browne: a life in pictures* (Dublin, 1994).

—, *Father Browne's Australia* (Dublin, 1994).

—, *Father Browne's Cork* (Dublin, 1995).

—, *Father Browne's Dublin* (Dublin, 1996).

—, *Father Browne's England* (Dublin, 1996).

—, *L'Irlande du Pére Browne* (Paris, 1996).

—, *Father Browne's* Titanic *Album* (Dublin, 1997).

—, *The last days of the* Titanic (Colorado, 1997).

—, *Father Browne's* Titanic (Tokyo, 1997).

—, *Titanic postcards* (Dublin, 1997).

—, *Images of Aran: photographs by Father Browne* (Dublin, 1998).

—, *The Jesuits in Dublin* (Dublin, 1999).

—, *Father Browne's ships and shipping* (Dublin, 2000).

—, *Father Browne's Tipperary* (Dublin, 2001).

—, *Father Browne's trains and railways* (Dublin, 2004).

—, *Father Browne's Limerick* (Dublin, 2005).

—, *Father Browne's Galway* (Dublin, 2006).

—, *All our yesterdays: Father Browne's photographs of children* (Dublin, 2007).

O'Dowd, Anne, *Common clothes & clothing, 1860–1930* (Dublin, 1990).

Osborne, Chrissy, *Michael Collins: a life in pictures* (Cork, 2007).

Patterson, E.M., *The Lough Swilly railway* (Belfast, 1988).

Pearson, Peter, *Dublin city and citizens – a photographic celebration* (Dublin, 1988).

—, *Between the mountain and the blue sea* (Dublin, 1998).

Perez, Michael, *The focal encyclopaedia of photography*, 4th ed. (New York, 2007).

Pochin-Mould, D., *Ireland from the air* (Belfast, 1972).

Philips, Charles & Alan Axelrod, *My brother's face: portraits of the Civil War in photographs, diaries and letters* (San Francisco, 1993).

Pols, Robert, *Family photographs, 1860–1945* (London, 2002).

Radley, Seán, *Picture Millstreet: a photographic profile of Millstreet, 1880–1980* (Cork, 1997).

Reilly, James M., *Care and identification of 19th-century photographic prints* (Rochester, NY, 1986).

Rosenblum, Naoimi, *A world history of photography* (New York, 1984).

Rouse, Sarah, *Into the light: an illustrated guide to the photographic collections in the National Library of Ireland* (Dublin, 1998).

Rynne, Colin & Billy Wigham, *Forgotten Cork: photographs from the Day collection* (Cork, 2004).

Sexton, Seán & Christine Kinealy, *The Irish: a photohistory, 1840–1940* (London, 2002).

Shaw, Rose, *Carleton's country* (Dublin, 1930).

Shields, Stan, *Stan's Galway* (Galway, 2006).

Somerville-Large, Peter & Jason Hawkes, *Ireland from the air* (London, 1996).

Sontag, Susan, *On photography* (New York, 1977).

—, *At the same time* (New York, 2007).

Squiers, Carol (ed.), *The critical image: essays in contemporary photography* (Seattle, 1990).

Tagg, John, *The burden of representation: essays on photographies and histories* (Minnesota, 1988).

Trachtenberg, Alan (ed.), *Classic essays on photography* (New Haven, CT, 1980).

—, *Lincoln's smile and other enigmas* (New Haven, CT, 2008).

Tyers, Padraig, *Ceanara Chorca Dhuibhne: cnuasach griangraf, 1888–1960* (Dún Chaoin, 1991).

Vergara, Camilio José, *American ruins* (New York, 1999).

Walker, Brian, *Faces of the past: a photographic and literary record of Ulster life, 1880–1915* (Belfast, 1974, repr. 1999).

—, *Sentry Hill, an Ulster farm and family* (Belfast, 1981, repr. 2003).

Weaver, Mike (ed.), *Henry Fox Talbot: selected texts and bibliographies* (Oxford, 1992).

Whitmarsh, Victor, *Shadows on glass: Galway, 1895–1960* (Galway, 2003).

Index

This index does not include the photographic collections in the book.
They are listed in alphabetical order in chapter 3 above, pages 52–84.